(PS B
lawyer!
destiny!)
D1090156

For Alia,
Brilliant, generous
& discerning. Your
talents will change the
world. Keep your heart
open & know that the
angels root for you every
day! You will change the
world. You already have!
Love, Paula
Frangee

West Academic Publishing's Law School Advisory Board

JESSE H. CHOPER
Professor Of Law and Dean Emeritus,
University of California, Berkeley

JOSHUA DRESSLER
Professor of Law, Michael E. Moritz College of Law,
The Ohio State University

YALE KAMISAR
Professor of Law Emeritus, University of San Diego
Professor of Law Emeritus, University of Michigan

MARY KAY KANE
Professor of Law, Chancellor and Dean Emeritus,
University of California,
Hastings College of the Law

LARRY D. KRAMER
President, William and Flora Hewlett Foundation

JONATHAN R. MACEY
Professor of Law, Yale Law School

ARTHUR R. MILLER
University Professor, New York University
Formerly Bruce Bromley Professor of Law, Harvard University

GRANT S. NELSON
Professor of Law, Pepperdine University
Professor of Law Emeritus, University of California, Los Angeles

A. BENJAMIN SPENCER
Professor of Law,
Washington & Lee University School of Law

JAMES J. WHITE
Professor of Law, University of Michigan

Being a Law Student

A Daily Companion for Law School, Practice and Life

by

Paula A. Franzese
Peter W. Rodino Professor of Law
Seton Hall Law School

Creator and Editor of the Short and Happy Series

WEST
ACADEMIC
PUBLISHING

Mat #41562423

The publisher is not engaged in rendering legal or other professional advice, and this publication is not a substitute for the advice of an attorney. If you require legal or other expert advice, you should seek the services of a competent attorney or other professional.

Short and Happy Guide Series is a trademark registered in the U.S. Patent and Trademark Office.

© 2014 LEG, Inc. d/b/a West Academic
  444 Cedar Street, Suite 700
  St. Paul, MN 55101
  1-877-888-1330

Printed in the United States of America

ISBN: 978-0-314-29107-3

For Michael Luigi and Nina Paula, the song in my heart.

Preface

This is a book of messages that I have shared with my students over the past three decades. I am a law professor and public interest lawyer, and I teach Property, Commercial Law, Civil Rights and Civil Liberties and First Amendment Values. Inspired by the generosity and kindness of my students, I also teach about hope, compassion, being proud of who you are and where you come from, service and our responsibility as healers. I am grateful that my message has struck a responsive chord.

This book endeavors to allay some of the fears that law school, work and life can conjure up. Amidst tides of cynicism, it is a reminder to include goodness and kindness in everything that we do. Legal education can sometimes divorce humanity and our own humanness from the study and practice of the subject matter at hand. That tendency is tragic. Lawyers are not automatons, technicians or hired guns. We are people, representing people in need.

When we separate virtue from learning we miss the point. When we hide or segment off whole aspects of our selves to become something we think we are supposed to be we lose our integrity. The very word *"integrity"* comes from the Latin *integritas*, meaning wholeness. We live with integrity when we are able to integrate the pursuit of excellence with the steadfast commitment to decency. We live with integrity when we respect intelligence, but respect kindness more.

The law can take its practitioners to great heights. But no matter the altitude, the vision that we embrace for our craft should include a view of the law as both noble and honorable. It is a perspective that urges us to wake from the slumber of complacency and recognize that we are all healers.

We heal with our words and with our actions. In the face of seas of need, we heal with one kind thought and one generous impulse rendered one day at a time. We heal when we resolve to love the law, and to treat it as if we love it. We heal when we love the clients and constituencies that we are lucky enough to serve. We heal when we finally decide to love ourselves so much that the spillover cannot help but bring joy to the world.

This book was inspired by and written with great love. My students are shining lights. I thank them for the privilege.

Paula A. Franzese

February, 2014

About the Author

Paula A. Franzese, the Peter W. Rodino Professor of Law at Seton Hall Law School, is the creator and editor of the *Short and Happy Guide* series, and is the author of *A Short and Happy Guide to Property* and *A Short and Happy Guide to Being a College Student*.

Nationally renowned for her excellence in teaching, Prof. Franzese is the unprecedented ten-time recipient of the Student Bar Association's Professor of the Year Award, has been named "Exemplary Teacher" by the American Association of Higher Education and most recently was named one of only 26 "best law teachers in the United States." The book, *What the Best Law Teachers Do* (Harvard University Press), profiles in detail the pedagogical approach that renders her a "dazzlingly effective model of rigor, hard work, creativity and humility".

Professor Franzese has demonstrated and deconstructed her pedagogical expertise on teaching as both art and science at workshops and colloquia across the country. She is the Gilbert's "*Legend of the Law*" in Property (West audio series), the national Property lecturer for the BAR/BRI bar review course, the author of the book *Strategies and Techniques for Teaching Property* (Walters Kluwer) and a contributor to the books *America's Second Gilded Age? Perspectives on Law and Class Differences* (NYU Press), *The Affective Assistance of Counsel: Practicing Law as a Healing Profession* (Carolina Academic Press), and *Reaction and Reform in New Jersey* (Hall Institute).

Professor Franzese's scholarship in the area of Property law includes critical examination of common interest communities, homeowners associations and the dilemma of privatization, the law of servitudes, exclusionary zoning, affordable housing, adverse possession doctrine and takings law. She joined in the submission to the U.S. Supreme Court of an *amicus* brief in the *Kelo* Case, and has written and presented on takings law reform.

Professor Franzese is a Fellow of the American College of Real Estate Lawyers, a Fellow of the American Bar Foundation and the recipient of numerous accolades, including the Sir Thomas More Medal of Honor, the YWCA Woman of Influence Award, the Women Lawyers Association's Trailblazer Award, and the State Bar Foundation's Medal of Honor.

As one of the country's leading experts on government ethics, Professor Franzese has spearheaded ethics reform initiatives on behalf of three governors, serving as Special Ethics Counsel to Governor Richard Codey, Chair of the State Ethics Commission, Vice-Chair of the Election Law Enforcement Commission and as ethics advisor to state and local governments across the country, including Mayor Cory Booker's administration in Newark. Among her initiatives in those arenas, she and Justice Daniel J. O'Hern promulgated the Uniform Ethics Code, a pioneering statutory achievement that has become a model for national replication.

In recognition of her accomplishments on behalf of good government, Professor Franzese was presented with the National Council on Governmental Ethics Laws (COGEL) Award, the highest form of recognition conferred by the organization, in honor of her "significant, demonstrable and positive contributions to the fields of campaign finance, elections, ethics, freedom of information and lobbying over a significant period of time."

Professor Franzese was a litigator with Cahill, Gordon, and Reindel in New York City, where she also served as a member of the New York Housing Court Reform Project and the Governor's Task Force on Life and Law. She clerked for Justice Alan B. Handler of the New Jersey Supreme Court.

Professor Franzese received her B.A., *summa cum laude*, Phi Beta Kappa, from Barnard College, Columbia University, where she was awarded the Bryson Prize, Alpha Zeta Fellowship, Marion Churchill White Prize, Davidson-Foreman Foundation Award and Barnard Alumnae Fellowship, and her J.D. from Columbia University School of Law, where she was an International Fellow, Teaching Fellow and recipient of the prestigious Rosenman Prize for excellence in public law courses.

Table of Contents

PART 7. HOW TO SUCCEED ON EXAMS AND WHAT TO DO WHEN YOU FEEL WORRIED, UNSURE OR A FLOP AT THE TASK AT HAND

PART 8. HOW TO PERSIST IN YOUR CAPACITY TO LOVE THE LAW

A Short & Happy Guide to Being a Law Student

Introduction

Why and When to Read This Book

Law school and the practice of law can be the most wonderful experience, but its rigor can also bring moments of doubt, even for the most self-assured. People who are accustomed to feeling competent and successful can suddenly find themselves questioning their abilities and their place in new territory. The night before I was to begin law school, I remember phoning home in a panic. I still had more than fifty pages to read, and I could not understand most of it. Tired and overwhelmed, I cried to my dad, *"I'm terrified. I don't think that the law is for me. I can't do this."* My father replied, *"Paolina"* (his pet name for me, which translated from Italian is said to mean *"little legal genius of our nation,"* although that may be a loose translation), *"Throw your fears out the window. For this moment, stop thinking with your weary mind and go to what you know in your heart. You are precisely where you are meant to be."* Then my dad added three words that I have invoked on many occasions since: *"GO TO SLEEP!"*

Most fears are born of fatigue, and a good night's rest is often curative. This book is meant to be a nightstand companion whenever anxiety or dread starts to creep in and whenever the voices of the naysayers ("You can't do this," "It's too hard," "What's the point?") start to take up space in your head. Make one of its chapters the last thing you read before turning in for the night. Make parts of it the first thing you read upon rising. It contains messages of hope and it will remind you of the mightiness of your mission and the magnitude of your abilities.

We suffer because we forget. Remember who you are and where you come from. Your parents, grandparents, their parents and ancestors before them struggled, sacrificed and triumphed so that you would have the opportunity to be where you are at this very moment. The hard work has already been done. The table has been set. All you need to do is take your seat, respectfully and with great humility but also with the presence of mind to know that you belong here, you will thrive here, and you will use your life to bear living witness to the legacy of virtue that preceded you.

PART 1

You Are Going to Be a Lawyer. Be Excited and Feel Proud.

Law school will teach you a method of analysis and hone your powers of discernment so that you can and will become a ninja for the good.

Your admission to law school represents a significant achievement. You have begun the most exciting time of your intellectual career. Law school is challenging and exhilarating. The practice of law presents many opportunities to do well and, even more essentially, to accomplish good. Feel proud and privileged that you are here. The law is a powerful instrument. You are on your way to becoming a wielder of that instrument.

CHAPTER 1

Dreams Brought You Here. You Are Now Making Them Come True.

The world is yours.

Education is the great equalizer and knowledge is power. No matter your beginnings, you are now firmly on the road to making your dreams come true. That sets you apart from the countless souls who find themselves stuck by circumstance and life choices. Your world is limitless. Your course is still unwritten and your path is ripe with promise. That promise of a better life may not yet be available to the guy sitting next to you on the train today, or the woman sitting across from you in the laundry room. You are one of the lucky ones. Across the world, countless people will never get the chance that you have now. You are creating something for your sake and for theirs, and it is very good and very important.

Your degree will equip you to use the rule of law to advance the cause of progress.

With your law degree, you will have the opportunity to effect change. Change is needed. There is too much brutality in the world. As an educated citizen of the world conversant in the legal method, you will have a skill set that will give you credibility and access. Therein resides your chance to be a paradigm shifter, to bring peace where there is acrimony and understanding where there is intolerance. You will learn to use the rule of law not in pursuit of "win at all costs" ruthlessness but to promote the cause of progress and equal access to justice for all.

The most significant lawyers and law students value the gentler virtues. They know that wisdom and compassion are indivisible.

You do not need to be aggressive or competitive to succeed. Play your game, no one else's. Your true nature is virtuous. If you stray from your true nature to try to become someone or something else, you will lose your way. Stay true to yourself. Continue to value and practice generosity and compassion. Speak to the better instincts of the people who come into your life. The goodness in you is the same goodness in them. By your example, you will help them to remember.

Whenever you come to a crossroads, choose the path with integrity. Do not demean yourself by responding to meanness in kind. Believe in the virtue of others, even when they are not showing their virtuous selves. Treat people as they could be, and in time they will meet you there.

You will teach others that kindness comes from strength.

The decision to lead with both your mind and heart won't always be easy. In the days ahead, sometimes your virtue will be mistaken for weakness. But you will know better, and by your example you will help others to see that kindness comes from strength.

It takes courage to step away from the crowds and stand up for what is right. It takes character to stand up for the underdog. In a world where incivility can seem the norm, it takes steadfastness of purpose to refuse to participate in another's attempt to demean or denigrate anyone else. Be firm in your resolve to be the voice of compassion. Decide now who and what you will stand for.

You will decline the opportunity to answer low-mindedness with more of the same. You will take the high road, again and again, knowing that the force of moral authority will rise up to meet you there. From that perch, the change that you want to see in the world will come.

As a lawyer, you are uniquely trained to ordain positive outcomes and alter the course of history for the better.

The study of law is the study of justice. As such, it presents a most enduring foundation on which to build a life of significance. Without justice, there is no hope. And there can be no justice without just lawyers (thank you Shavar Jeffries). You are now on your way to becoming a just lawyer.

The law is a noble profession.

No matter what you may have heard or read to the contrary, the law is a most noble profession. With your degree, you will have the opportunity to effect positive change. As a lawyer, you will become conversant with the rule of law and the art of dispute resolution. Therein resides your chance to advance the aims of progress.

Think about the great paradigm shifters throughout the course of human history—Sir Thomas More, Thomas Jefferson, Abraham Lincoln, Mahatma Gandhi, Barbara Jordan, Sandra Day O'Connor and Nelson Mandela to name a few. All were lawyers.

The best lawyers understand that while *"compassion without technique is a mess, technique without compassion is a menace."*

Karl Llewellyn, a legal giant and architect of so much of the modern law of Contracts, made that astute observation. Every lawyer who has advanced the cause of rightness has done so by committing to the relentless pursuit of excellence as perceived through a loving lens.

History tells of the atrocities committed at the hands of technocrats whose actions were devoid of any moral referent. Still, some will advocate that aggression, domination, control and self-interest are what it will take to succeed. Reject that assessment. To the extent that it has held sway, it helps to explain why the reputation of our craft has suffered.

Never hesitate to speak to the better instincts of the clients, colleagues and constituencies who will soon come into your life. Seek to introduce wisdom, even in the midst of what seems like chaos, and compassion no matter the adversity.

Our profession offers many choices. When you find yourself having to make one of those choices, take the virtuous path. Your decision to do that, repeatedly exercised, will have an impact far beyond any courtroom or boardroom victory. In turn, your example will free others to emulate the wisdom of your choices. Like a pebble in a stream, you will never know where your influence stops.

A good lawyer defies the push of the crowds and takes a stand for decency.

With your law degree, you will be well-equipped to stand up for the underdog. Starting now, as a lawyer-in-training, if you see someone being victimized by another's meanness or unfair treatment, say something. Get in the way of the bully's brand of brutality by calling it out for what it is—cowardice. Decide that you are a leader, not a follower. Never allow your partnership with anyone or anything to cause you to become complicit in the hurting of another. Never allow your partnership with anyone or anything to cause you to become complicit in the hurting of yourself.

You will lead with both your mind and your heart.

The decision to integrate virtue into all that you do won't always be easy. Sometime you will suffer disappointment and feel like an island. Particularly then, know that you are never ever alone. All people of substance, present and past, are cheering for you, rooting for you and here to catch you when you sometimes stumble. Count on the tradition of goodness that preceded you. Know that you walk with kings and queens.

CHAPTER 2

You Are Smart Enough to
Be in Law School

Genius is overrated.

If you are feeling intimidated by law school, you are most likely presuming that your classmates must be so much smarter than you, your teachers are all geniuses and "the law" is so difficult that only the smartest people are able to understand it and work with it. All of that is nonsense and you need to get it out of your head right now.

Avoid any and all comparisons with others.

What you bring to this pursuit is what only you can bring. The life experiences that led you to this moment are yours alone and they have prepared you well. Comparison is disrespect for yourself and the object of your comparative appraisal. It cannot help but have you thinking that you are "more than" or "less than" someone else. That sort of conclusion is both presumptuous and false. Do not denigrate your unique glory by comparing it to another's.

Moreover, your snap judgments about another's strengths or weaknesses are most likely wrong. Resist the urge to label people. Kierkegaard got it right when he said, "*If you label me, you negate me.*" Stop sizing up your classmates in some misguided attempt to determine where you stand. You are no better than and no worse than anyone else. Everyone has a story to tell and something to teach you. And you have your own story to tell and something to teach the world.

You are smart enough to be in law school.

At first, some the legal terms that you are reading will seem foreign and it will take you a long time to get through a case. Take your time and know that what you are experiencing everyone is experiencing. Give yourself several weeks at least to begin to get the hang of the legal method. While the methodology may be new, the skills that you need to succeed—reading, critical thinking and analysis—are the same skills that got you here.

When you start to feel overwhelmed or less than worthy, realize that you are most likely holding yourself to a crazy standard of perfection. Abandon the quest for some brand of nuanced excellence and simply commit to "good enough." As long as your performance in class, on the exam, the moot court exercise or the legal writing assignment is good enough, you will be fine.

To finish the race is to win the race. You do not have to come in first, second or even in the top 99%. The last one to cross the finish line still crosses the finish line. At your first trial, no judge will ask how you did in moot court. At your first closing, no client will pause to ask your Property grade. Every finish brings you closer to the dream. Take your time and cross the line.

The smartest is the one who works the hardest.

There are "brilliant people" devoid of decency and "geniuses" without the guts to get the job done. They find themselves relegated to the ranks of the reviled or forgotten. As we were growing up, my mom told us time and again, *"The smartest is the one who works the hardest."*

Work hard and push the ball up the mountain one inch at a time. Persist in the commitment to work hard and you will reach the mountaintop and stay there. Not because you were so smart, but because you were smart enough to know that true greatness comes because of your persistence, strength of character and stubborn commitment to the cause of the good.

There is a force that meets good with good. That force will give you the push when you need it and carry you when you grow weary. It is rooting for you, not testing you. It is cheering you on, every step of the way.

Intelligence is multi-dimensional. You will find your brand of genius and create your own artistry within the law.

Do not measure your success according to some linear numerical calculation. That one-dimensional marker cannot begin to know your own unique brand of excellence, what it is that you will excel at most and how it is that you will truly shine. As time goes on, you will discover particular aptitudes of yours that you never knew you had. Those are your brand of genius.

To uncover the *virtuoso* inside of you, say yes to every opportunity that law school presents, whether in the clinics, on a journal, with moot court, in student government, on behalf of a community leadership initiative, as a judicial intern, a *pro bono* volunteer, a mentor and the list goes on. Through a process of elimination, you will come to know what makes your heart sing.

The Majesty of the Law and Your Place in It: Ten Reasons to Be Really Happy About Becoming a Lawyer

REASON ONE: Law school will teach you a method of analysis and hone your powers of discernment so that you can and will become a ninja for the good.

Be excited, because the law is a wonderful profession. No matter your ultimate career aspirations, the study of law and the mastery of the legal method will allow you to be a game-changer, whether in the arenas of social justice, politics, business, diplomacy, journalism, international affairs, technology, corporate management, medicine, health care, human resources and the list goes on.

When the naysayers try to conjure up some parade of horribles about our craft, return to any one or all of the following points. Each tells the truth about the profession that you are joining and the professional that you are becoming.

REASON TWO: The law is a magnificent career path. It will allow you to do well and, most essentially, to find meaning in the work that you do.

A career in the law can give you every material gain that your heart desires. It will also give you the greatest gift of all—a life of meaning. That meaning comes when you realize that you are learning and someday will be practicing all that you have learned for a purpose mightier than yourself.

We do not live only for ourselves. You have come to this place and time to serve. You are connected to the whole of humanity and soon you will be uniquely trained to humanize the inhumane and give voice to the silenced.

Your life will grow in meaning as you move away from ego-driven motivations and toward purpose-driven aspirations. You live your life on purpose when you live for the betterment of others. You live a life of honor when you decide to care more about your significance than your success. Be glad because you have committed to a course of study that will afford you success **and** significance.

REASON THREE: We are a society of laws. When people are in trouble, most often it is trouble with the law. We are the fixers, the handlers and the rule of reason's last best hope.

As lawyers, we use our expertise to come walking into the room just when it seems to our clients that everyone else has walked out. Our presence on the scene brings a sigh of relief and often with one phone call, one appearance or one meeting we can make things better. The law degree vests us with an imprimatur of legitimacy, expertise and authority that commands attention. Our phone calls are returned and our messages are heeded. You are growing in stature, using your newfound status as law student and lawyer to command the right kind of attention.

We use our power responsibly when we decide to be givers of hope. By training, we are equipped to be champions of the underdog, protecting from the tyranny of the majority. We may not always be popular, but when we do our job well, justice will be served. You are now building the fortitude of mind and heart essential to the task at hand. You are becoming a just lawyer.

REASON FOUR: Wisdom and compassion are indivisible. You will become a virtuous lawyer.

Your greatness will reside in your capacity to stubbornly adhere to your virtue and generosity as your continue to hone your intellectual acuities. You are becoming a virtuous lawyer.

REASON FIVE: As you grow in expertise and stature, you will teach that each of us is no better (or worse) than anyone else.

Arrogance and one-upmanship have no place in your circle of first principles. Avoid comparisons with others. Do not chase dreams that are not your own. Know that everyone has a story to tell and something to teach you. I remember listening to an interview of Bono, the musician and lead singer of the band U-2, on the occasion of his receipt of a lifetime achievement award. He was asked what it felt like to be so great. His answer went something like this: *"We're just a bunch of musicians waiting for God to come walking into the room. Only then do we become the instruments for greatness."* You are becoming an instrument for greatness.

REASON SIX: You will learn to honor the art in you, and not you in the art.

Leave your ego at the door because, at bottom, the journey that you have begun is not about you. It is about the countless people, most still nameless and unknown, who are waiting for you to get on with the task at hand so that the art that is in you might be used to make their lives better. You will experience the joy of giving your expertise in service to others. In so doing, you will bring many rewards, satisfaction and joy to your own life.

REASON SEVEN: You will help the clients and constituencies that you serve to be governed by what inspires them, rather than what makes them feel small.

You are learning to harness the power of your mind to think about and talk about everything that is good, honorable and right with the world and your place in it. As a lawyer, you will have the stature to teach others to do the same. Your life will move in the direction of your predominant thoughts. Be vigilant about them. Think often of all that you are thankful for. When a thought that makes you feel bad seeps in, you can choose another thought.

REASON EIGHT: You will learn to trust that every day you will be found precisely where you need to be.

Spirit responds to the willingness to serve. You will come to know and trust that as you seek to be used for a purpose mightier than yourself, you will be found precisely where you need to be.

Ask for ways to use your growing expertise to ease the pain of others. There is a force that greets the generous impulse with the means to achieve its fruition.

Every day, I ask God to find me where He needs me to be. When my time is short, I send up the prayer, *"Use me."* I invoke those two words as my shorthand for, *"I surrender my expertise to You. If there are words that need to be spoken today, give me those words. If there are deeds that You need done, put them in my path."*

Decide today that you will use what you are learning in service to others. Then watch what happens as you are placed precisely where you need to be.

REASON NINE: You will resolve to love the law, and to treat it as if you love it. You will promise yourself that you will persist in loving it, no matter the disappointments and occasional disenchantments.

Refuse to heed the cynics or the jaded. Do not listen to that voice in your head that sometimes wants to convince you that you cannot do this or that our profession is less than noble. That voice is a liar.

Proclaim out loud today and every day that you love the law, even if you have to fake it until you make it. Profess your love for law school, for the law and for our craft often and with great enthusiasm. Your life will mirror your level of rhetoric about it. Your experiences will rise or fall to meet your level of expectations.

When friends and family ask how it is going, reply, *"It is amazing. I am learning so much and building so many skill sets. My classmates are great people, and I learn from them every day. My professors are the best. I am developing muscles I never knew I had, and I will use this strength to make the world a better place. I promise you that. I won't let you down. I am going to make you proud."* They will smile and reply, *"You already are."*

REASON TEN: You will change your life by speaking only good things about it and others.

When friends and classmates begin to complain, try to help them to switch up the thought. If it becomes clear that you cannot do that, simply remove yourself from the conversation. Misery loves company. Refuse to be an accomplice to another's less than worthy words. You are learning to let what you say facilitate tolerance, understanding and hopefulness. Be excited about this day, because it is bringing you one step closer to the life of your dreams.

The Day I Fell in Love
with the Law

Committing to the greater good

As a new lawyer I worked on Wall Street, for the wonderful law firm of Cahill Gordon & Reindel. The very talented attorneys and firm leadership there encouraged us to take on *pro bono* public interest initiatives when we could, and I eagerly heeded that invitation. Soon, I was part of a housing court reform project and later an affordable housing initiative aimed at preventing the wholesale conversion of subsidized apartments into luxury condominiums. A team of lawyers, politicians and administrators from New York City government gathered to assess options and determine how best to accommodate the needs of the working poor families of lower Manhattan while recognizing the promise of economic revitalization for the area.

We would meet every Tuesday and often, at the close of those meetings, I would find myself feeling frustrated at the bureaucratic machinations of those in power and the snail's pace of progress. On one of those Tuesday nights I phoned home, principally to complain and to vent. My dad answered, and I began my litany of grievances: *"Daddy, the politicians aren't listening to me. Maybe it's because I'm young, or maybe because I'm a woman. Everyone seems mired in their own agendas and they aren't committed to the people behind the issues. There are real families whose futures are at stake here. Where will they live if this doesn't get resolved in their favor? But this committee doesn't care about that. This committee. . . ."*

Right there, mid-sentence, my dad interrupted me. He had heard enough and he refused to be an accomplice to my collection of grievances and perceived victimization. Instead, he said, *"Stop. You are focusing too much on what you are not getting, and not thinking enough about what you are not giving. Whatever is missing from this effort is whatever you refuse to give it. What is it that you have not yet brought to the table? You speak of the families whose lives hang in the balance. Have you met those families?"* I answered that I knew of them only on paper. He replied, *"Go and meet them. Bring your committee to meet them. Let their stories set the course for your group's work."*

"Where there is no love, put love, and you will find love."

I thought about the words: *Whatever is missing from any effort is whatever you refuse to give it.* Then I remembered the words of St. Paul, words that I had actually selected as my "favorite quote" for my high school yearbook photo: *"Where there is no love, put love, and you will find love."* Instead of infusing the task at hand with love—love for the constituencies that we were privileged to serve, love for the promise of justice, love for the humanness and humanity of the enterprise—I was infusing it with limiting judgments and ego-driven indictments. I realized then what had to be done.

Rather than dwell on what I detested—the politicization of the process—I reached out to the legal services attorneys on the committee whose example I admired. Together we organized a tenants' meeting at the building whose continued existence was threatened by the gentrification effort. We arranged to have our committee's next meeting become a part of that larger gathering of the affected tenants. There, the fear and worry of the residents, many of them parents to small children, became real. We heard from a mom who was holding down two jobs at minimum wage and struggling to make the monthly rent, from a young man whose new job finally took him off the streets and into a place to call his own, and on it went. In those stories, we came to know the point of our work, why it mattered as much as it did and what, as the lawyers, we needed to do.

"You have some really good lawyers on your side."

At the end of that long night, as were heading for the door, I heard a voice calling, *"Lawyer."* I turned around and saw a boy, maybe ten or eleven years old. I said, *"Hey buddy, you're up so late."* He said, *"I'm here with my mom, and she is worried. You're going to help us, right?"* I smiled and said, with as much conviction as I could muster, *"Yes. Tell your mom not to worry. You have some really good lawyers on your side. It is going to be fine."* At that, I watched as the boy exhaled. I actually saw him breathe a sigh of relief. That is the moment when I fell in love with the law. That is the instant when it occurred to me that the words *"You have some really good lawyers on your side"* could relieve suffering and give the greatest gift of all—the gift of hope.

"There can be no justice without just lawyers."

That encounter represented the moment when I went from an ego-driven to a purpose-motivated life. I was not going to get sidelined or distracted by dwelling on petty slights or perceived disrespect. I was no longer a collector of grievances, looking for ways to be right about my harsh judgments of others. The enterprise at hand was not about feeding my ego. It was about the clients and constituencies whose lives hung in the balance between justice and its absence. As my colleague and civil rights champion Shavar Jeffries has said, *"There can be no justice without just lawyers."* I was determined to be a just lawyer.

That resolve is what I had been withholding from our committee's work. Now, I brought it, and I was met at that place of commitment by similar-minded champions. The resources that we needed showed up. The system started to work on our behalf. The building was saved from conversion and its tenants were safe.

There is a force that meets good with good. Love the law and treat it as if you love it. Love the cause of justice. Love the clients, constituencies and colleagues put in your path. Resolve now to be a just lawyer. Define yourself as a giver of hope. Be the voice for those yet to find their own. *"Where there is no love, put love, and you will find love."*

PART 2

For Law School and Life, Five Guideposts to Live By

- *Remember who you are and where you come from. You stand on the shoulders of giants, and you vindicate their sacrifices by living the promise they foresaw.*

- *Remember Whose you are. You are never alone.*

- *Be mindful of the power of your words. Declare right now that you love the law and its practice. Your life will match your level of expectation.*

- *Be of service. The surest way out of your pain is to help others out of theirs. The best way to grow in stature is to help others grow in theirs.*

- *Have an answer to the question "who do you think you are?" You are a champion of the underdog, a voice for those yet to find their own, a giver of hope and a game changer for the greater good.*

CHAPTER 5

The First Guidepost: Remember Who You Are and Where You Come From

We suffer when we forget the victories of our histories. Remember who you are and where you come from. Your parents, grandparents, their parents and ancestors before them struggled, sacrificed and overcame so that you would have the opportunity to be where you are at this very moment. The hard work has already been done. The table has been set. All you need to do is take your seat, respectfully and with great humility but also with the presence of mind to know that you belong here, you will thrive here, and you will use your life to bear living witness to the legacy of virtue that preceded you.

In law school and in the practice of law, stay close to the people who love you the most, who believe in you and who will be there to remind you of the song in your heart.

Most suffering comes when we forget the triumphs of our histories. I remember where I come from when I think about the struggles of my parents and the challenges that our family endured growing up poor in Brooklyn, New York. My dad, an Italian immigrant without the benefit of a formal education, could find work only on the docks, as a longshoreman. Even working overtime, the wages made it hard to pay the bills. I remember the shame that my mom felt when the electric company turned off our power, and the dread that came when the landlord would pound on the door because the rent was late.

My parents endured the indignities felt every day by the working poor. My dad's own hopes of becoming a lawyer were squashed by the exigencies of circumstance and poverty, but he understood that education could be a great equalizer. He and my mom worked so that their four children might one day have a better life anchored in the opportunities that a professional degree could provide. My parents' calculation was correct: Each of us went on to earn advanced degrees, and we now enjoy a quality of life that my parents dreamed of. As we have grown in stature, we pay it forward every day. Actually, we have grown in stature because we pay it forward every day.

"You are not what you are called. You are what you answer to."

As a little girl, I remember looking through my dad's union book. At the time, my dad joined the effort to unionize the workers so that conditions on the docks might be improved. That effort was met with strong resistance from management. An anti-union antagonist had scrawled some terrible ethnic slurs on my dad's book. I could not yet understand all of the words scribbled there, but I knew that they were meant to hurt my dad. I started to cry as I said, "Dad, we have to erase these words. You have to do something. You can't let them call you that." My dad replied, "I know that I am not what those words try to say I am. I am not that. And I will not erase those words because I want the person who wrote them to know that the work of progress will continue not because of his actions, but in spite of them."

Years later, one of my students sent me a photo of a wall inscribed with the words, "You are not what you are called. You are what you answer to." That was my dad's point.

We have the choice, every day, to decide what we will answer to. Remember that whenever someone tries to make you feel small. Turn to the people who love you the most when you need to be reminded of what you are and what you are not. Let them help you to decide what to answer to.

"Leave this one alone."

My dad's dreams of becoming a lawyer were lived through me. By the time I was a young law professor, my dad had become a chef of some renown (see Chapter 29 on How to Prepare Penne Vodka). On a humid Saturday in May, our entire family gathered for a birthday celebration. My dad prepared a feast, and as he cooked, I caught him up on the events of the week. I am the oldest of four children, and my dad reminded me to keep the youngest, my brother Louis who would soon graduate from law school, "on the right road." "My job is done," he said with great pride. I protested, reminding him that he was still young and had yet to see my younger siblings' get married, the birth of grandchildren and the countless milestones still to come. We changed topics as he threw in the pasta.

Later that evening, the smoke from the birthday cake's candles set off my dad's asthma. (He developed acute asthma during his time on the docks. This was before the advent of occupational safety regulations.) As a precaution, we decided to make a quick trip to the hospital to get him treatment and some relief. My mom encouraged the rest of the family to stay put. We would have the cake later.

By the time we got to the hospital, it became clear that matters had gone from bad to worse. I frantically screamed to the nurse on call, "Please help us. My father can't breathe." As I turned to face my dad, he whispered to me in Italian, "Leave this one alone." I burst into tears as I realized that he knew something, perhaps all day long, that I did not want to know. He would be leaving us on that day.

And so he did. Hours later, my mom, brother and I returned home to the cake still on the table. It was my birthday cake. It was my birthday celebration. My father always said that his life, the life that mattered, began the day he became a dad. Somehow, by choosing this day, the anniversary of the first day of his becoming a dad, he was telling us that his journey was completed. Even his final counsel to me, "Leave this one alone," told me everything I needed to know. All my life, I have been my parents' fiercest advocate and my family's champion, the lawyer-in-training and then the attorney fighting for their rights. This time, there was no argument to be made, no cause to advance.

It is now many years later, and still I return to those words to help me to know when to dive in and when to wait at the dock, when to take up a matter and when to let it be.

Today, say what needs to be said to the people you love the most.

On the occasion of my dad's funeral, each one of his four children took up the task of giving testimony to the life that he lived. I began with the words of Carlos Castaneda, as told in one of the Don Juan allegories. There, the elder sage turns to the younger man, who is filled with the hubris and arrogance of youth, and quietly says, "The trouble with you is, you think you have time."

Do not succumb to the delusion that you have all the time in the world. The time is now to love with all of your heart. Today, at this very moment, say what needs to be said. Write a letter of gratitude to the person or persons whose sacrifices have so much to do with the opportunity now in your hands.

As you grow in stature, tend to your roots

This world is yours. As you continue to grow, tend to your roots. Let them nourish you and ground you in the bedrock of your first principles. Remember who you are and where you come from.

Hold tight to your ideals, your goodness and your commitment to exalting the kinder virtues. When the naysayers pop up to shake your resolve, stand firm and remember that you never, ever stand alone.

All who have come before you, who believe in you and who have so much to do with your being where you are at this very moment are holding you, guiding you and lighting your road. To lose your sense of self because of defeatist ideas, or as a consequence of the assessments of others, is to disrespect their legacy. Never give up. You are more talented than you know, and the best is yet to be.

There is an ancient proverb that says, "To get to the fruit of the tree, you must go out on a limb." Get out there on that limb, the branch that bears the name of honor. Know that below you there will always be a safety net, composed of the arms outstretched and interlocked of all who have loved you, who respect you and who stand strong and ready to catch you if and when you sometimes fall. Those people are here for you now, whether in body or in spirit. Count on them. While they are here, love them with all your heart. When they leave this place and time, know that they carry you. Love does not die.

You stand on the shoulders of giants, and you vindicate their sacrifices by living the promise they foresaw.

CHAPTER 6

The Second Guidepost: You Are Never Alone

You do not live by yourself or solely for yourself.

You are never alone. You are a child of God, and the divinity in you is the divinity in all. Let your life bear living witness to the power of transcendence. Each of us is better than the worst thing we have ever done. No one is beyond the promise of redemption and the virtue in some can be ignited in others.

Herman Melville was right that countless threads connect you to the brilliant tapestry of the whole of humanity. You belong to a community whose sum is even more magnificent than any of its parts. To serve that community you are now preparing your mind and spirit. You will be a champion of the underdog, a crusader for justice and a voice for those who have yet to find their own.

Remember that you do not live solely for yourself. What you are accomplishing now you are achieving for the countless clients and constituencies, most as yet nameless and unknown, who will be counting on you to make the difference that only you can make. You will be their giver of hope.

Trust that *"there is a star that you are under, put there for a reason."* You are precisely where you are meant to be, and life is rooting for you every step of the way.

In law school and in life, the most important question is not *what* you want to be, but *who* you want to be.

Take some time now to arrive at your set of first principles—the virtues that inform the person you want to be. How do you want to be thought of? What do you want said about you? The characteristics that you want to embrace should include generosity, kindness, virtue, honesty and the commitment to excellence. Let your first principles be guided by the recognition that you are in the world but not *of* it. Your source transcends the limitations of this place and time and it is vast, loving and beneficent. This is a compassionate universe. It does not test us. It cheers for us.

To stay within your circle of first principles, commit to the practice of relentless gratitude.

Be the most grateful person in every room. Look for the nobility in all people and in all things. Recognize that this moment will never be here again. Say what needs to be said in the pursuit of unyielding appreciation.

Ask to be used for a purpose mightier than yourself.

If you send up only one prayer every day, make that prayer *"Use me."* Those two words demonstrate your willingness to be a vessel through which good and noble work can be done. They will help you to stay on purpose, and they will assure that you are always found where you need to be.

Divine guidance responds to the slightest whisper, whether in the form of *"use me"* or *"help me."* Not too long ago and far from home, I was lost on my way to a concert. A young woman appeared out of nowhere and had the compassion to say, *"You seem lost. May I help you?"* I explained where I needed to be, and she was kind enough to reply, *"That's hard to find from here. I will walk you over to the concert hall."* As we walked, and without knowing anything about me, she told me that she was finishing her undergraduate studies and that her dream was to go to law school. She was the first person in her family to pursue that ambition, and she was hoping to find a mentor. I told her that she just had. She is now my mentee, and just as she graced my path, I can now grace hers. On that occasion, both she and I were found where we needed to be.

Practice forgiveness.

Sometimes people will hurt you, whether unintentionally or, worse, on purpose. Forgive them. Be informed by their actions but by no means diminished by them. That means that you will be smart enough to protect yourself from further trespass and wise enough to know that while the transgressor's actions speak volumes about him or her, they do not speak for you.

People can be cruel and reckless. You will forgive for your sake. You will forgive because you refuse to be weighed down by the boulder of resentment. You will forgive because you value yourself enough to stop hurting yourself because of what someone else did.

CHAPTER 7

The Third Guidepost:
Be Mindful of the Power
of Your Words

Your life will move in the direction of your most dominant rhetoric about it.

Choose your words carefully. Let what you say facilitate the cause of peace and understanding. Speak only good things about people, even when they have not yet caught up to your level of expectation for them. They will. Centuries ago, the German philosopher Goethe observed, *"If you treat an individual as he is, he will remain how he is. But if you treat him as if he were what he ought to be and could be, he will become what he ought to be and could be."*

Stop saying mean things about yourself.

Be disciplined with your self-talk. Do not be your worst critic. When you look in the mirror, what are you saying to yourself? When you make a mistake, how badly do you berate yourself?

Would you ever think of being that unkind to another? Show yourself the same generosity that you so readily extend to others.

Rather than listen to your inner monologue, talk *to* yourself. Be your own cheerleader and your own coach. For guidance on what your self-talk should sound like, imagine that a six year old child is always following you, watching your every move and listening to your every thought. Suppose that everything that he or she will come to know about the world and his or her place in it will come from what he or she hears from you. What would you want that child to hear and to believe? **Be that.**

You are enough.

Stop holding yourself to some external model of perfection. It is an illusion. When you begin to be unkind to yourself, imagine that very innocent child standing beside you, bearing silent witness to your self-directed brutality and internalizing it. Is that what you want to teach?

When the voices of doubt creep in—*"You can't do this," "You're not that smart," "You're ugly," "You're fat"*—interrupt them in their tracks and declare firmly, *"I am enough."*

You do not have to be perfect, or anything close to the distorted standard that the "smart police" or "beauty police" would have you internalize. All of that is sleight of hand and digitized fakery.

The two questions to ask at the end of each day.

At the end of each day, ask yourself two questions. *First, did you try to do your best?* If you got into the ring, no matter that you might have gotten clobbered once there, it was a good day. Tomorrow, with a fresh start, you will enter once again, stronger and wiser. Getting knocked down is not what counts. *What matters is getting back up.*

Second, did you bring love into the world? If you brought a smile to someone's face, made another's load lighter, sowed seeds of kindness or stirred the pot of compassion, then no matter what you think you looked like or sounded like, regardless of the number on the scale and irrespective of anyone else's critique, *you were beautiful.*

Declare right now that you love the promise of the law.

You might be thinking, *"But I haven't started law school yet,"* or *"But I'm not sure yet if I like the practice of law or not."* None of that matters.

Hear me now and believe me later: Your life will meet you at your level of expectation for it. What that means is, even if you have to fake it until you make it, you should begin, right now, to enthusiastically declare your passion and admiration for the promise of the law and its potential to change lives (including your own) for the better.

Starting now, relentlessly extend gratitude to every single person on your path.

In school and at work, say thank you on a daily basis to everyone whose efforts contribute to your day, from the security guard at the front desk to the cashier in the cafeteria to the classmate or colleague seated next to you to the professor instructing you to the judge addressing you to the janitor emptying the wastebaskets to the stranger who will soon be your friend.

Be the most grateful person in every room. Think about what a child does when you give him a really great gift. As he jumps up and down for joy, what are you thinking? Maybe, *"I love this child. And I want to give him more!"* Be that child. Your immense gratitude for the good in your life will bring you even greater good.

The people that you meet will rise to your level of expectation for them.

Prepare to love your classmates, teachers and colleagues. That preparation has very little to do with them, and everything to do with you. Your experiences will rise (or fall) to your level of expectation. Your life will take you in the path of your predominant thoughts and words about it.

Whenever you think a good or positive thought about another, say it out loud!

We tend to find it easier to criticize than to praise. That may be a conditioned response, or simply a way to avoid our vulnerability. Sometimes we decline to tell people the positive things we think and feel about them for fear of being thought a phony or a fake. But trust me on this: Our lizard brains—even the most primitive parts of our cerebral functions—can spot authenticity a mile away. We know sincerity. When you say what you mean, truthfully and with kindness, you will not be misunderstood.

If you think that a classmate made an excellent point in class, tell her. If you admire the statesmanship of a student leader on campus, tell him. If you strive to emulate the example of a particularly generous friend, tell her. If you are on the bus and you notice that the driver greets every passenger with courtesy and respect, compliment the driver. If a salesperson is doing a great job under pressure, say so out loud. There is so much that is negative and toxic out there in the marketplace of ideas. Do not leave the high-minded and positive observations unsaid.

When you seek out the good in others, and then proclaim that good to them and about them, you bring good to yourself. There is a Chinese proverb that states, *"A bit of fragrance always clings to the hand that gives you flowers."* What you do for others, you do for yourself. What you do *to* others, you do to yourself. Take care then in all that you put out into the world, for it cannot help but return to you.

Sometimes, no matter that you have professed your love for the law, it will feel as though it does not love you back.

It takes courage to decide to love the law, your classmates, your teachers, colleagues and friends. To love is to risk disappointment. But choose love anyway. Sometimes the law and its practice will break your heart. But know that a broken heart has more room.

Some days will be harder than others. Especially then, emerge from the rubble of a bad grade, a letter of rejection or a dismal moot court performance and stand even taller than you did before. It did not kill you. It made you stronger. Dig in your heels, become the stubborn person that you know you can be, and declare, *"But I still love you, and the best is yet to be!"*

Greatness will be yours *not* because you never failed. Greatness will be yours because sometimes you did fail, *but still you persisted.*

You will succeed because even In the face of all disenchantment you remained anchored in your firm conviction that *the best is yet to be.* Refusing to join the chorus of cynics, you stuck with the choir of angels. And with that choice, you changed the world for the better.

CHAPTER 8

The Fourth Guidepost: Be of Service

The surest way to allay your own pain is to help others find ways out of theirs.

Decide now that wherever your professional path takes you, you will use your expertise to ease the suffering of others. Keep that as your aim, and the opportunities to serve will find you.

There is much to be done. Too many are denied the effective assistance of counsel. Countless meritorious claims will never see the light of day. In the midst of rising seas of need, you will do what you can with the time that you have. And that will make all the difference.

Look for the starfish now in your hands.

There is a parable of a child on the beach. The tide precipitously pulls out, leaving thousands of starfish stranded on the shore. If not thrown back, they will dry up and die. The boy begins picking them up, one at a time, and casting them back to sea. A passerby sees this and says, *"There are too many of them left here. What you're doing doesn't matter."* The boy looks down at the starfish in his hand—the starfish whose life he is about to spare—and replies, *"But it does matter to this starfish."*

Every act of generosity matters. There will be many starfish on your journey. Seek the wisdom to see what needs to be seen and the courage to respond with big-heartedness. Vow to share your emerging bounty of influence. There are many people, most still unknown to you, who have been waiting for you to earn this degree so that you can change their lives for the better. You will not let them down.

Listen to your mother.

My mom, Mary, has the biggest heart in the world. She lives in Brooklyn and works in Manhattan. Invariably, whether she is talking with her neighbors or overhearing others' conversations, she learns of someone's struggle with the law or the legal system. It might be a woman worried because she received an eviction notice, a man denied his dialysis because he is no longer insured, a single mom whose wages have been garnished because she defaulted on a loan or a student who made a mistake and is now in trouble with the authorities. Irrespective, my mom engages in a kind of reverse ambulance-chasing as she approaches the individual, whether friend or stranger, and says, *"My daughter Paula is an attorney and a law professor. She will help you for free."* My mom then gives out my card, and urges that the soon-to-be client call me.

Throughout my career, I have received countless phone calls as a result of my mom's generosity. Sometimes they come at the most inconvenient times. Sometimes I want to yell at my mother. But I always say yes. Yes, I will help you, or yes, I will find the right person to help you, and yes, I promise to follow up and no, I won't forget. I have been privileged to have spearheaded some significant legislative and policy reform throughout my career, but my most meaningful work has come because my mom taught me to see the starfish.

See what needs to be seen and respond with compassion.

On your way to and from school or work every day, notice the people who come into your path. Is there a homeless man at the train station? Is there a woman at the crosswalk who seems very sad? Is there another student or colleague on his way to the parking garage who looks like he has had a really hard day? Snap out of your own preoccupations, turn off your phone and see what needs to be seen. Do what you can, with whatever resources you have, to make the day better for that person.

Decide every day that you are going to make someone's day.

Set as your intention: *"I am going to make someone's day today."* Equip yourself to be able to do just that. Keep an extra sandwich in your backpack to give to a person who seems hungry. Carry in your pocket a $5.00 gift card to McDonald's or Dunkin' Donuts or some other local eatery and give it to someone who could really use it. Initiate a conversation with the person who seems distressed and brighten his or her mood. Sometimes all it takes is a kind word of encouragement to take a person from blue to better.

For your birthday and on special occasions, when family and friends ask what you would like, ask for bunches of $5.00 gift cards and explain why. That will inspire others to follow your example, and like a pebble in a stream, the ripples of your kindness will extend out.

I began that practice in college. Still today, I carry gift cards, small bills and some food wherever I go. The week before Thanksgiving, I keep with me more substantial gift cards to supermarkets and as I perceive need, I give them away. At Christmastime, I bring wrapped toys to school and dispatch my students to find worthy recipients. They are my accomplices and I am theirs in the joy-spreading scheme.

When you ask to be used for a purpose bigger than yourself, you will be heard and your request will be answered. Simply show up, and the opportunity will appear.

When you decide that you are going to use this day to be a giver of hope, you become a game-changer. With one generous impulse rendered one day at a time, you become a paradigm-shifter. Your goodness will shake people out of their cynicism and despair and make them question whether they are right about their harsh judgments of the world. When they try to convict humanity, *you will be their basis for reasonable doubt.*

Most of all, your assiduous commitment to the good of others will make your life beautiful. *You will be a midwife to the birth of hope*. I have had the privilege to watch as hope has sprung from the most desolate places. My life has never been the same.

Super Bowl Sunday

Several years ago, on Super Bowl Sunday, I stood at the express checkout line of our local supermarket behind a dad and his young daughter. The little girl was about 6 years old, and the dad looked worn down. Their cart was small and contained only essentials—milk, eggs, bread—and one indulgence, a festive little cake shaped like a football and brightly decorated. The dad was very carefully watching the screen as his items were rung up and it became clear that he needed to be sure that he had enough in food assistance coupons to be able to pay for the transaction. When it came time to ring up the cake, the dad realized that he was out of funds. He set the cake off to the side and told the cashier that he would not be purchasing it. I watched the little girl's face, and my heart broke.

I had to do something, but I did not want to embarrass or humiliate the man. I had a twenty dollar bill in my hand to pay for my items. I quietly let that $20 fall to the ground. Then, I tapped the man on the shoulder and asked, *"Did you drop that?"* He looked down and said, *"No, that's not mine."* I picked up the bill and insisted, *"No, I think you dropped this. It's not mine, and I thought I saw it fall from your pocket."* Our eyes locked, and in that instant he realized what I was doing. With grace and a soft thank you, he took the bill, and asked the cashier to add the cake to his order. The little girl hugged her dad and then practically hugged the cake.

In the years since that day, I have never again seen that man. But I carry him and his daughter in my heart. They are there whenever I begin to wonder if what we do matters. I can hear them whisper, *"It does."*

As you learn, teach others.

In school and in practice, you will be learning so much. Share your newfound knowledge. Go back to your local high school, middle school or grade school and meet with the principal. Indicate your willingness to give a talk to interested pre-law students, to be a mentor and to help with a civics curriculum. I teach *Loving the Law,* an elective class, to middle school children in my hometown. I deputize the students to be "agents of positive change." I teach about good citizenship and the promise of our living Constitution. Guest speakers, experts in their fields, visit us each week to teach about family law, finance, criminal procedure, personal injury law, negotiation, employment law, animal welfare law and more.

The best way to learn something is to teach it. You will grow in expertise as you summon the courage to get out there and share your expanding repertoire of knowledge with the world.

The Fifth Guidepost: Have Your Own Answer to the Question: *Who Do You Think You Are?*

When you decide to be a person of principle, invariably others will ask, "*Who do you think you are?*" Have your own answer to that question. Do not let the world answer for you.

Go back to your circle of first principles. *That is who you think you are.* You are a child of God and a citizen of the world. You belong to a community greater than yourself. You are a person of integrity. You are a champion of the underdog, a crusader for justice and a voice for those who have yet to find their own. Most of all, you are a giver of hope. You live your life knowing that the divinity in you is the divinity in all of us. Each of us is better than the worst thing we have ever done. No one is beyond the promise of redemption.

This is a compassionate world. It will not test your perception of yourself. It will take you at your word and when your word is good it will cheer you on. It will greet your generous impulse with a sigh of relief and allow the path to meet you at your level of intention.

Your experiences will mirror back to you the intentions behind your actions.

Let what you do be consistent with who you think you are. Be clear about your intentions before you act. Intend to be an agent for positive change. Intend to heal the pain of others. Intend to proclaim the virtuous. An intention will always return to its source.

You are a champion of the underdog.

My son Michael played basketball in school. In the sixth grade, he came home from a game dejected. He told me that the other team lost, but not because they were outplayed. They lost because more than half of the team did not have suitable footwear. Michael noticed this during play, as some of the boys were tripping and skidding on the court. Their sneakers were frayed, without laces or adequate soles.

My son was dismayed at the injustice of it all. How could it be that the kids did not have basketball shoes? I explained that maybe their families could not afford them. *"What can we do?"* he asked. I answered that he had already done half the work. He had chosen to see what needed to be seen. Now, together we could be part of the solution.

We decided to start a sneaker fund. The next day I mentioned the effort to my class, and with characteristic generosity my students rose to the occasion. Bake sales were held and donations solicited. Without being asked, my son contributed some of his birthday money. Soon, we had more than we imagined. I called the school's principal with the good news. She was overjoyed. She put me in touch with the Athletic Director. He couldn't believe it. With the donation, he was able to buy uniforms for the team and outfit each player. He sent us a picture of the team in their beautiful green and gold uniforms with a note that my son keeps on his bulletin board to this day.

You are a voice for those who have yet to find their own.

My children will not abide meanness. A new boy joined my son's seventh grade class, and as a newcomer the child had a hard time fitting in. Seizing on his vulnerability, some of the other students began making fun of him and excluding him from recess activities. My son saw this, and did not like it. He described how, during the daily football game, that boy sat alone on the school steps. Apparently some of the other players had made plain that they did not want the new boy slowing down the game. My son Michael took a stand, and said, *"If he doesn't play, I don't play."* Michael walked off the field, and sat with the new boy. They talked and Michael learned that the boy was learning how to weld, and that he could create art from melted metal. He could even take some of the objects that he made and, with his mom, create greeting cards.

Michael and his new friend continued their recess talks until one day the invitation was extended for both of them to join the game. Mike said to his buddy, *"If you're in, I'm in."* Together they played, and soon the new boy was part of the crew.

Later that year, Michael wanted to celebrate his birthday with a sleepover at our house. He invited every boy in the class. The party was a big success, and at the end of the night I went downstairs to check on everyone. All of the boys were asleep, except for the new boy. He was sitting up, simply looking around the room. I asked him if everything was ok, if he needed anything or if he was homesick. He replied, *"No, it's not that. I'm just happy. I'm trying not to fall asleep because I want to remember this day."*

The next week a card arrived in the mail, addressed to our family. It was from the new boy and his family. The card featured a beautiful piece of art that the boy had welded. At the top were the words, ***"No act of kindness is ever wasted."***

PART 3

Preparing to Be Happy in Law School, at Work and in Relationships

Commit to the practices outlined in this section to be your best in school, at work and in relationships. Check in with its pages often. They will provide a safe harbor in sometimes stormy seas.

CHAPTER 10

Arrive At Your Set of First Principles

You want to be a person of integrity.

It is important that you take some time now to think about the virtues and values that matter most to you. Those are your first principles, meaning the code that you live by. They are the moral compass by which you chart your course and comport your behavior.

When your words and actions are in accord with your first principles, your life will run smoothly. When what you say and what you do departs from your first principles, you will veer off course. When that happens, as it sometimes will, the quickest way to get back on track is to remind yourself that you are a person of integrity and that you will make the adjustments and the amends that a person of integrity would make to get back to good.

Decide now what you stand for. What is the highest and best expression of you? How would you want to be remembered? What will your legacy be? What are you willing to enter the room for? What are you willing to walk out for?

Think of your first principles as a circle. When your behavior keeps you within the circle, you are in the flow and you feel good. When your actions are outside the circle, you feel guilt, that nagging tug at your conscience. That is your signal to get back in the circle.

No matter that you will sometimes stray from it, always return to your center of virtue. Do this for the sake of others, and for your own sake. **In a world of infinite possibilities, you will not get what you want.** *You will get what you are.* The law of reciprocity is always at work. We get what we give. We are denied what we withhold. Thus, *give what you want to receive.*

Be clear about your first principles. Write them down. Refer to them often. They will be your safe harbor against the changing winds of time.

Finish these sentences: *"These are the central values on which I base my life: _____."* *"These are the attributes I admire most: _____."* *"This is how I hope others would describe me: _____."* Write down the answers on an index card. Use that card as a bookmark when you begin school or a new job. Refer to it often. It will help you to keep your head on straight, especially when others seem to be losing theirs. We suffer when we stray from our first principles. We find relief when we return to them.

Before I began law school I did this exercise. I jotted down the answers on an index card, and I kept that card on my bulletin board, where I would see it every day. Here is what I wrote on that card:

"I value intelligence and I respect kindness even more. I stand for the realization of equal access to justice for all. I believe in the promise of redemption and the

power of love. I admire the relentless commitment to excellence when it is practiced with compassion. I seek to emulate those who stay above the fray, whose high-mindedness has no room for the petty or mean spirited. I want to be remembered for seeing the good in everyone, because it is there."

Everything that you say and do begins with an intention. Keep your intentions consistent with your first principles. That way, you assure not only your success, but also your significance.

Integrity is when the outside matches the inside. You live a life of significance when your words and actions are virtue made visible.

Integrity is present when you talk the talk *and* walk the walk. You live a life of integrity when you speak the truth compassionately rather than brutally. There is too much brutality in the world already. You lead with integrity when you say what you mean and mean what you say. You practice integrity when you are able to integrate the pursuit of excellence with the steadfast commitment to decency. You demonstrate integrity when you respect intelligence, but respect kindness more.

To separate virtue from your professional pursuits is to risk losing your soul. To segment off whole aspects of yourself to become something you think you are supposed to be is to lose your integrity.

You live with integrity when you bring all of you—artist, scholar, musician, teacher, student, parent, scientist, lover of literature, athlete, chef and the list goes on—to your endeavors.

You contain multitudes. Let others see the brilliance of your many facets. The very word *"integrity"* comes from the Latin *integritas,* meaning wholeness. To integrate all that you are into all that you do is to lead with integrity.

There is no room for duplicity or phoniness in a life lived with integrity. There is an absence of honor whenever you say something *to* a person but something quite different *about* that person. You will feel the consequences of any duality or inauthenticity that you participate in. Your conscience will tug at you and you will feel like a fraud. That feeling will diminish your power in the world and erode your sense of self. Hence, for your own sake as well as for the sake of all others, declare right now that you will live a life of integrity.

We all hope that the people we look up to *are really like that.* One of my students once told the class of the time that she was in the audience of the Oprah Winfrey show. The first question the class asked was, *"What is she really like?"* (She is wonderful.) Our higher instincts are vindicated when we are able to validate that the generosity or valor that we perceive to be present in another is indeed there. Our lesser instincts are fed by the tabloids, blogs, social media thugs and gossip-mongers whose aim is to convince us otherwise.

Stay away from the bottom-feeders and traffickers in human frailties. Stay above the fray.

When someone starts to gossip, you have several high-minded options. First, simply walk away. Extricate yourself from the conversation. Second, say to the person, *"You are better than that. We all are."* Then, change the topic. Third, help to correct the speaker's perceptions. That is the most powerful way to respond. If you know the person that is the target of the hurtful speech, speak about the goodness and virtue that you know she possesses. If you do not know the person well or at all or if it has been difficult for you to arrive at a positive estimation of him or her, be the voice of compassion by simply stating that as she lives and learns she will do better.

When using the internet, do not let the anonymity of a comments section entice you to write something that is simply not worthy of you. Use social media responsibly. (See Chapter 13: How to Use Social Media Responsibly). Let your digitized imprint be principled, generous and positive. Proclaim what you are *for* instead of decrying what you are *against*. If you read a post that is mean-spirited, privately message its author to indicate how and why you think he or she ought to be self-corrective.

Live your life so that those who know you best see your best.

Recently, an esteemed judge counseled our law students to *"love your work and work at your love."* In law school and in the practice, do not neglect the people who matter most to you. Tend to your most precious relationships. Show up for the people you love, and let them see not just the stressed you but the best of you.

At social occasions, my children are often asked by my students and colleagues, *"Is she really this nice at home?"* One of my greatest moments came when I overheard my daughter reply, *"No. She's nicer."* Live your life so that the person you are at home is even more generous than the person the world sees.

Your life will move in the direction of greatness when what you say and what you do is reliably consistent with who you want to be.

You will grow in power and stature as your daily habits comport with your first principles. Strive each day to keep your words and actions within your circle of core values. When you find yourself acting outside the circle, be self-corrective. Apologize, make amends and forgive yourself. Make the adjustments that you need to make to get back to center and then move forward. Stop re-living the incident that took you off track. Stop *"should-ing"* on yourself, as in *"I should have done this"* or *"I shouldn't have done that."* You are human, and if you had nothing left to learn you would be dead.

Do not live a neutral life. Decide what you stand for.

Take a stand for decency, fairness and the cause of justice. Stand on the side of virtue. Stick up for the underdog. Be a voice for someone who has yet to find his own. In the presence of cruelty, do not be impartial. There is a well of courage inside of you that you have not even begun to tap. Go to that well and draw from it. Call out meanness and wrongdoing. Speak your peace truthfully and with dignity, *but speak your peace.* To remain neutral in the presence of injustice is to stand for nothing. Complacency is the enemy of the good.

Call out bullying for what it is—insecurity disguised as force.

Defy the push of the crowds and take a stand for justness. If you see someone being victimized by another's wrongdoing, say something. Get in the way of the bully's brand of brutality by interrupting it in its tracks. Bullying is weakness disguised as force.

Decide that you are a leader, not a follower. Do not become complicit in the hurting of another.

Speak passionately about what you stand for, rather than what you stand *against.*

What you resist persists. Let your life be directed by what you admire, rather than what repulses you. When Mother Teresa was asked to attend anti-war rallies, she always declined. *"Ask me to attend a pro-peace rally,"* she would reply, *"and I will be there."* The great game-changers of history knew that we grow in power and stature when we decide to firmly stand *for* something, rather than *against* something else.

CHAPTER 11

How to Stay Within Your Circle of First Principles

To stay within your circle of first principles, habituate three practices: 1) *Say thank you countless times a day*, 2) *Be of service in all settings* and 3) *Forgive generously*.

Say thank you countless times a day.

A heart that is grateful does not have room for meanness or pettiness. Say thank you when you see a thing of beauty. Say thank you when you observe an act of kindness. Even say thank you when you observe someone behaving badly because you are grateful to know what not to do.

One afternoon, as I was leaving the law school's parking lot, I stopped to ask the attendant, Bernadette, how she was. She replied, "*I am blessed to be in the day.*" That is a perfect statement and a perfect response. No matter how the day is going, you are lucky enough to be in it.

You are still here. That means that you have another chance to make new choices. If the day is bad because you argued with someone, reach out and apologize, even if it was not your fault. You can be right or you can be happy. Choose happiness. Then say thank you because you took the high road.

If the day is less than great because you are tired, find the time to take a nap. Make that a priority. Do not underestimate the need for rest. Then say thank you because you found a place to rest.

If the day is hard because you are simply not at your best, know that everyone has off days and let it go. Then say thank you because tomorrow is going to be a better day.

Whenever things start to go wrong, stop the trajectory of doom in its tracks and declare firmly, *"No! This is not how the day is going to go."* Then immediately shift your focus from whatever just went wrong to everything that is going right. Step away from the computer screen and find someone to hug. Send flowers to make someone's day. Put on *Pharrell* and dance with your dog. If you are stuck in traffic, begin praying for the drivers to your left and to your right. Your day will move in the direction of your focal point. Focus on the good in your midst and the good to come.

Be of service in all settings.

Make every context in which you find yourself less about you and more about how you can be of service. Seek out ways to help. At the start of each day, declare that your intention is to make another's load lighter. Leave your ego at the door of every room that you are about to enter, and generously do something so that the room is better because you were there. That might mean mopping the floor or speaking kind words, baking for someone or making someone laugh. No matter the form that it takes, be of service.

Generously forgive.

Do not be a collector of grievances. They will only clutter your closet. Give everyone the benefit of the doubt, and stay above the fray. Let go of your resentments. There is a Native American wisdom that *"it is not the miles ahead that wear us out. It is the grain of sand in our shoe."* Do not let another's transgression wear you down. Shake out your shoe and keep moving forward.

We stray from our core values when we seek revenge or when we decide that we need to tell anyone who will listen about the misdeed that has us so agitated. When someone hurts your feelings, take it up with him or her and no one else. Do not enlist the sympathy of others and do not give the matter a life of its own by spreading it around. That sort of behavior will reflect poorly on you and it may burn bridges best left intact.

"No tree has branches so foolish as to fight among themselves." (Ojibwa Indian Wisdom)

Do not fight with your family members. Be at peace with your friends. For that matter, endeavor to construe family broadly. We are one family of lawyers, one family of Americans, one family of world citizens and one family of humanity. Generously construe your version of "us" so that "us" versus "them" conceptualizations yield to the essential truth that we cry the same tears.

CHAPTER 12

Ten Ways to Make Wise Choices

In school, at work and in life, you will be the sum total of the choices you make. This chapter contains a set of do's and don'ts to help you to make wise choices.

1) Choose your friends carefully.

To know a person, meet their friends. That means that people will make assumptions about you based on who you study with, who you socialize with and who you are closest to. Surround yourself with friends, classmates and colleagues who share your first principles, believe in the importance of living with integrity and care about their futures. Study with people who are serious about doing well in school. Socialize with people who are generous, kind and understand the consequences of stupidity. Embrace your inner nerd. It is ok to be a nerd and, later on, to marry a nerd. Nerds tend to rule the world.

2) Leave any relationship that makes you feel small, demeaned or denigrated.

Abuse only escalates over time. If you are with someone who calls you names, get out of the relationship. If you are with someone who is jealous of your success, get out. If you are with someone who tries to keep you from your family and friends, get out. If you are with someone who tries to control you, get out. If you are with someone who hits you, even once, get out. Once is too much, and it is never only once. No matter the tears and apologies, get out and do not look back. Love yourself enough to set healthy boundaries. You are no one's punching bag (figuratively or, God forbid, literally). You are a person of goodness and substance and you deserve to be treated that way. *Treat yourself that way, and trust that the world will come to follow your example. You will meet your match.*

3) Study hard and work hard.

When studying, turn off your cell phone, use your computer only for studying or work purposes, and do what needs to be done. The child inside of you will try to get you to take frequent breaks or find things to do that are more fun than the work at hand. Have a talk with that child and say, *"Listen, we have to study for the next two hours. But after that, we will watch a movie"* (or play a *video game, go shopping, eat ice cream, take a walk or whatever else you know would delight you.)* Then, be sure to keep your promise. If you do, you will observe amazing results as your inner six year old learns to trust your word and frees you to get done what needs to be done, in anticipation of the reward at the end of the task. You will instantly feel more energized and focused.

4) Do not let a bad day or a bad grade go to your head.

If today was not your day, remember that it is *the day that was*. Like a puppy that gets caught in the rain, shake it off and move on. The good news is that tomorrow you get another opportunity to be better, stronger, wiser and kinder. No grade has the power to define you, chart your course or set your limits. Only you have that power. Decide that the world is yours, and it is.

5) If you drink, drink only in moderation.

Do not come to rely on alcohol as a way to be less socially awkward or as a means of fitting in or checking out. If your friends insist that you join them in drinking to excess, find new friends. If that seems too drastic a response, then muster the courage to set healthy boundaries. Eventually, friends worth having will respect your choice.

6) Never drink and drive.

Having even one drink on an empty stomach could set you up for a driving under the influence charge. That charge has serious consequences and it creates a permanent record subject to disclosure for the rest of your life. It has to be disclosed on bar admission applications and job applications. It will stigmatize you and haunt you. Do not get behind the wheel if you have been drinking.

7) Never get into a car where you suspect that the driver has been drinking.

Your life will be at risk. Others' lives will be at risk. Moreover, anyone reckless enough to get behind the wheel when cognitively impaired has bad judgment, and that poor judgment no doubt spills over into other aspect of that person's life. You do not want to be friends or in a relationship with a train wreck. You do not want to be in a vehicle that gets stopped, only to be searched with that search yielding contraband. No matter your innocence, you will be brought into the police precinct and suffer the untoward consequences of "guilt by association."

8) Never text and drive.

The temptation to do so is great, particularly at a red light or on a vast, empty expanse of road where the risk seems small. Resist that temptation, because when you are behind the wheel, no risk is small. *When you get in the car, put your phone out of reach.* It can wait. Countless tragedies have occurred because too many drivers succumbed to the illusion that they could send out a quick text while keeping their eyes on the road. That is a physiological impossibility. It could kill you and it could kill someone else. If you live and you did harm because you were texting and driving, you will go to jail. In a growing number of states, criminal liability can also attach to a person who knowingly texts someone who is driving.

9) Do not post inappropriate words or photos on your social media sites.

Your digital imprint will be scrutinized by prospective employers, colleagues, co-workers, adversaries and actual as well as potential love interests and their families and friends. Before you post or tweet anything, remember that you are an officer of the court. You are held to a higher standard. Keep what you say high-minded. Avoid overexposure in the photos that you post. Aim to be a class act. What you share online can and will reach lots of unintended recipients and some creepy viewers. Be discrete and be modest about what you choose to share.

10) Take care in what you choose to watch, read and listen to.

Avoid brutality in all its forms. Its images are haunting and have the potential over time to skew your perspective and desensitize you to the suffering of others. Retain your capacity to be shocked and appalled, so that you can respond with the power of your convictions and, when it is appropriate, the force of rightful outrage.

CHAPTER 13

How to Use Social Media Responsibly

Clean up your social media accounts.

Once you begin law school, you are a lawyer-in-training. As a lawyer, you are an officer of the court and a fiduciary for the clients that you serve. As such, you are held to a higher standard. Right now, go through your Facebook, Twitter, Instagram, Snapchat and Tumblr accounts and delete any photographs, posts or other communications that would place you in a bad light. Revisit the internet addresses that you have ascribed to your on-line accounts. Make sure that they are professional.

Prospective employers, current employers, potential clients, actual clients, co-workers, colleagues, adversaries and countless others will be checking your virtual footprint before making decisions that could affect your life. Further, in order to be admitted to the bar you must pass the Character and Fitness Committee review. You do not want any inappropriate or unseemly depictions attached to your name. In these new media times of ever-intersecting circles of influence and exchange, the personal cannot help but inform the professional. Take charge of the impression that your digitized patterns create.

Keep every communication to your professors, classmates, employers, co-workers and colleagues professional and high-minded. Never hit *send* in anger.

Expect that every electronic submission that you send can and often will be forwarded to others, including unintended recipients. When you communicate with a professor, employer or colleague by e-mail, keep the tone respectful and professional. If you have to miss a class, write in advance, explain and apologize. If you were in class and missed the attendance sheet, write to apologize and ask if the record can be amended to include note of your presence.

In class, if you are confused about some part of the subject matter, say so clearly but also with humility and deference. For example, state, *"I am so sorry to bother you with this, but I am having the hardest time understanding the rule against perpetuities. Here is what I think the rule means _____.* *Am I correct in that understanding?* Another example, *"I have read and re-read the Lopez case, but I am still struggling with the Court's holding. Would it be possible for me to come by this week to talk with you about the case and how it fits into our class discussions?"*

Avoid colloquialisms and an informal tone. Do not place the burden of your confusion on your professor, colleague or adversary when you write asking for help or clarification. For example, do not write, *"For the life of me I just don't get what we did in class today. Maybe you could explain it again in class tomorrow?"* Instead, try, *"As I review my notes, there are a few points that*

I'm afraid I don't have down yet. Would it be ok if I came by office hours later this week?"

If you are writing to another to vent or complain, don't.

Your electronic communications can and will be shared with others. Do not text or e-mail what you can say in person. If there is a problem that must be addressed in writing, keep your tone dispassionate and impeccably professional. Know that electronic communication leaves little room for the reader to discern nuance or tone. Do not try to be funny in your correspondence. Do not try to be sarcastic or caustic. It will not work, and most likely will backfire. Avoid derisive predicates such as *"what in the world?"*, *"how could you possibly?"* or *"what were you thinking?"*

However You Characterize School, Your Work and the People in Your Life, You Will Be Right

Whether you love or detest school, your job and the people in your life, you will be right. Life will meet you at your level of expectation. Expect great things.

Twenty years ago, anticipating the birth of our son Michael, we made plans to move from Manhattan to Cedar Grove, a small town that we did not know much about and that our friends and family had never heard of. When people asked, *"How do you feel about the move?"* I set aside all trepidation and replied, *"I am thrilled. I love our new neighborhood. I love the people who live there."* It did not matter that I had not yet met our neighbors. I was prepared to love them, not look for their faults. Sure enough, two decades later, we are still in the same house, we love our community and we adore our neighbors. Still today, as new neighbors move in and I am asked, *"How are they?"* I reply, irrespective of whether I have yet met them, *"They are wonderful. You will love them."* And I am right.

Recently my twelve year old nephew Louie was sitting at our kitchen table and asking if I happened to know anything about a new faculty member who was joining his school. *"Yes,"* I answered, *"She is fantastic. Make sure that you introduce yourself to her because she will be a great resource to you and you will learn so much from her."* Louie asked, *"When did you meet her?"* When I replied, *"I haven't yet,"* his quizzical look was answered by his mom, my sister-in-law Diane, who said, *"Louie, you just learned the Aunt Paula rule."*

Give everyone and everything the benefit of the doubt.

The good in some can be the good in all of us. Sometimes people have not yet shown you their best. Be patient. Give everyone the benefit of the doubt and be stubbornly committed to treating others not necessarily as they are, *but as they could be.* People will rise or fall to your level of expectancy about them. When someone disappoints you, simply say to yourself, *"She wasn't in her right mind just then. She'll get back to good."*

Embrace a Forrest Gump-like view of the world and the people in it. Do not overcomplicate things. Be guileless and refuse to dwell on the negative. Stay positive as you focus on the good. When the cynics say, *"Well, that's just stupid,"* smile and reply, *"Stupid is as stupid does."*

Declare right now that you love the promise of the law, the experience of law school and your place in the practice.

You might be thinking, *"But I haven't started school yet,"* or *"The people here seem cold"* or *"My job is boring."* None of that matters. Hear me now and believe me later: **Your life will meet you at your level of expectation for it.** What that means is, even if you have to fake it for now, you should begin to enthusiastically declare your passion and admiration for everything about the legal education that you are (or are about to) receive and the job that you have (or will have). Your word is powerful, and the world will meet you at your word.

In school and at work, relentlessly say thank you to everyone who is a part of your path. Remind yourself often that this is not something that you have to do. *It is something that you get to do.* Remember how lucky you are to have been blessed with the intellect, strength of purpose and opportunity now in your hands. Be glad and be grateful. A grateful heart does not have room for fear, pettiness, resentment or cynicism.

CHAPTER 15

What to Do When You Start to Feel Intimidated or Inadequate

No matter how self-assured you are, every new venture can bring moments of doubt. Whether in law school, a new job or an unfamiliar social situation, even people who usually feel competent can begin to doubt themselves. Law school and the practice can be exhilarating, but at first the law's rigor can be intimidating. Know that *everyone experiences the same qualms.* Set forth below are suggestions for when the voices of self-doubt come up.

Remember that feelings are not facts.

You have two minds: rational mind and emotion mind. Your rational mind puts you in your right mind, or within your reason-based faculties. It affords clarity and the opportunity for discernment. By contrast, your emotion mind is often fear-based. It can be irrational, rash and misguided in its assessments. That is why emotions like anger (and even love) can make us stupid. We tend to think and act irrationally when emotions run high. Think about the euphemisms that you have heard before, *"He is a fool for love," "Love is blind" or "She went into a blind rage."*

In school and in the practice, you will know that you have gone from rational thinking to emotion-based thinking when you begin to speak in absolute terms such as, *"I will never get all this work done," or "No one likes me" or "I don't understand any of this."* All of those sweeping assertions yield to the truth about you and the circumstance at hand. None of them are factual. When your self-talk begins to devolve into those all or nothing characterizations, declare a time-out and say, *"Feelings are not facts. I know in my right mind that none of that is true. I will take a break now and then return to my right mind."*

Take a nap and, better yet, get a good night's sleep.

The night before I was to begin law school, I remember feeling totally overwhelmed by the readings that were assigned. The words on the page were in English (mostly), but nonetheless inscrutable to me. I still had more than fifty pages to read, and I could not understand most of it. Tired and overwhelmed, I phoned home and cried to my dad, *"I'm terrified. I don't think that the law is for me. I can't do this."* My father replied, *"Paolina"* (his pet name for me, which translated from Italian is said to mean "little legal genius of our nation," although that may be a loose translation), *"Throw your fears out the window. For this moment, stop thinking with your weary mind and go to what you know in your heart. You are precisely where you are meant to be."* Then my dad added three words that I have invoked on many occasions since: *"GO TO SLEEP!"*

I have come to learn that most fears are born of fatigue, and a good night's rest is often the best remedy. When thoughts of dread start to creep in or when the voice of your inner critic (*"You can't do this," "It's too hard," "What's the point?"*) starts to take up space in your head, ask yourself if you are exhausted. Chances are you need to rest. Take a break and take a nap. Be sure to get a good night's sleep, even if that means that you have to let your professors know that you are not prepared for the next day's class or you have to wake up earlier than usual to review something for work. You will be amazed at how much easier everything is when you are rested.

Neither law school nor the practice of law is meant to be run as a sprint. You are on a long and scenic walk. Taking time to rest is time well spent.

Remember that the smartest is the one who works the hardest.

My youngest sister Rosalie struggled in school. Her aptitudes were not the ones that are prized on standardized tests or traditional means of evaluation. Still, her work ethic was relentless. When it took her classmates an hour to finish a given homework assignment, Rosalie took three hours. When her friends would boast that a test was easy, Rosalie felt a familiar dread because for her, the test was hard.

As a child, teen and young adult, Rosalie would spend hours at the kitchen table, studying her heart out. When she became discouraged she would say to my mom, *"I'm stupid. I'm just not smart enough."* My mom would have none of that. She understood that intelligence is multi-dimensional, and that inside of her daughter was a form of genius not yet tapped. She would reassure my sister by reminding her that any "objective" criteria for gauging intelligence were impossibly flawed and that "being smart" in any absolute sense was beside the point. Genius is overrated. Irrespective of any test score, victory belongs to the person with the tenacity and strength of heart to sit at that kitchen table and do what must be done. *"The smartest,"* my mom would say, *"is the one who works the hardest."*

Today, Rosalie is one of the nation's leading educators. She has authored books on remedial education, is an acclaimed teacher and a champion for children with learning differences. With my sister Marianne and brother-in-law Lee, Rosalie runs a Montessori school in New York. She recently told us about a little boy in one of her classes. He felt great shame because school was harder for him than it was for his classmates. Rosalie worked with the child after school, fortifying his aptitudes and his spirit. On one such occasion, my sister had forgotten her eyeglasses. She mentioned that to her student. The little boy replied with great sincerity and esteem, *"Ms. Franzese, you don't need your glasses because what you need to see, you see with your heart."*

Surround yourself with words and images that inspire you.

Surround yourself with messages of hope to remind you of the mightiness of your mission and the multi-dimensional magnitude of your abilities. There is a star that you are under, and you are precisely where you are meant to be. Keep words of inspiration in places where you can see them regularly.

Return to the five guideposts set forth earlier in this book in chapters five through nine. We suffer when we forget. Remember who you are and where you come from. The people who preceded you endured hardship but persevered so that you would have the opportunity to be where you are at this very moment. Take your place in the great tradition of all who have struggled and overcome and know that you belong here, you will thrive here, and you will use your life to bear living witness to the legacy of virtue that preceded you.

Remember the two questions to ask at the end of each day.

First, no matter the result, did you try your hardest? If you did, that is good enough. If you did not, tomorrow is another opportunity to do your best. Maintain a wholesome discipline, taking the highs and lows in stride. The journey is long, and every step counts. When the task at hand seems daunting, take baby steps, *but keep moving.*

Second, did you bring love into the world? If you performed even one act of kindness and brought a smile to even one person's face, it was a good day. Rest assured that the best is yet to be.

CHAPTER 16

Prepare to Find the Teachers Who Inspire You and to *Be* Like the Teachers Who Inspire You

Student and teacher share a sacred trust.

In school and in the practice, you will have great teachers, good teachers and some not so good teachers. Respect them all. Introduce yourself. Get to know them, and give them a chance to get to know you. Tell your story—why you are here, what you care most deeply out, what has inspired you about the law and what your hopes and dreams are. Every teacher, guide and mentor, whether in class or at work, shares a sacred trust with you. Each of us has a bounty of influence, opportunity and goodwill that can bring you closer to the attainment of your dreams.

Emulate the teachers you admire.

Be governed by the example set by the teachers who inspire you. Do not dwell too much on those whose practices are less than exemplary. Your behavior will move in the direction of your most dominant thoughts. Stay high-minded and emulate high-mindedness.

We never forget the imprint left by the teachers who are able to fortify our minds and touch our hearts. No matter that you are now in law school or in the practice, keep close at hand the legacy left by your most precious teachers—the ones who believed in you, who raised your spirits and who demonstrated that no act of kindness is ever wasted. Carry those champions in your heart. Make them proud.

Mrs. Sylvia Romanick: Kindness made visible.

The first teacher to make me a better person was Mrs. Sylvia Romanick, my first grade teacher. She was kind, wise and good hearted. She taught us about compassion and generosity. With one glance, I loved her, and I knew that she loved all of us.

At home, I would speak of Mrs. Romanick every day. One night, my mom said, *"One day we should have Mrs. Romanick over for lunch."* Somehow, I took that to mean that *tomorrow* we *will* have Mrs. Romanick over for lunch. The next day, without confirming my understanding with my mom, I gleefully marched into school and said, *"Mrs. Romanick, my parents would like the pleasure of your company today for lunch."* My teacher was delighted, and at the designated hour we walked the one block home.

As we began climbing the stairs to my family's apartment, I yelled, *"Mom, Dad, Mrs. Romanick is here for lunch!"* It was not until years later that I learned that this had come as an immense surprise to both my parents. My mom had been tending to my little sisters and my dad had just gotten off his second shift and was ironing his shirt for his work later in the day. Still, without missing a beat my parents beamed as they said, *"How wonderful! We have been expecting you! We are going to make you the most delicious omelet!"* Omelets it was, and as we sat around that hastily prepared table I could not have been happier or more proud.

Mrs. Romanick was pregnant that year, and by March, at nine months, it was time for her to leave. My mom, knowing of my adoration, asked if I would like to give her a baby gift. I jumped at the opportunity and off to the gift shop we went. There I picked out a silver baby spoon. The shopkeeper asked if we would like the spoon engraved. My mom suggested that we put a little R on it, for Romanick. I said, *"No, let's put a little P on it, for Paula."* *"But,"* my mother responded, *"It's unlikely that the baby will be named Paula."* Somehow, that fact was irrelevant to me. Thus, the spoon came to bear my initial.

When I presented the P spoon to my beloved teacher she looked at the engraving and with characteristic generosity said, *"How wonderful! Every time we use this I will think of you!"* I began crying tears of joy mixed with tears of sadness, because already I was beginning to miss my teacher.

Since it was her last day, Mrs. Romanick asked if I would like to help carry her lesson plans to her car. I was overjoyed to do so, but when it came time to hug my teacher goodbye, it all became too much. I began sobbing, fell to the ground and held on to her ankles for dear life. As she tried to pry me loose, I threw up on her beautiful shoes. (I had a sensitive stomach and the meatball sandwich my mom had made for lunch followed by the Hawaiian Punch chaser did not help.) Mrs. Romanick never returned to teaching.

I share that story with my law classes with the fantasy that one year someone will stand and say, *"I am Roger Romanick, child of Mrs. Sylvia Romanick. I was the one who ate from the P spoon."* That day has never come, but something else even more magical did happen. As a law professor, when I was nine months pregnant with my first child Michael and it was time for me to say goodbye to my beloved class, my students presented me with a silver spoon set engraved in tiny letters with each of their initials. (Thankfully, they did not throw up on me.) I treasure those spoons to this day.

I sought out the Mrs. Romanick in each of my teachers for all of my remaining years as a student, and I seek to emulate her virtue and generosity now as a teacher myself. I have had exquisite teachers, and in their humanity I have found Mrs. Romanick again and again. Her commitment to excellence and decency found its greatest mirror in my treasured college professor and mentor, Peter Juviler.

Professor Peter Henry Juviler: Wisdom and compassion are indivisible.

It has been said that when the student is ready, the teacher appears. And so it was that I, an impressionable freshman at Barnard College, sat in Prof. Peter Juviler's political science seminar. Engaging, brilliant and most of all kind, he taught about the capacity of a few committed people to change the world. With characteristic humility, he never realized that he was the exemplar for all that he taught.

The greatest teachers, I think, are forces of nature; not in the form of a tornado but instead in the form of a persistent whisper on the fields of their students' potentiality. Prof. Juviler was whispering to each of us, *"Stretch, expand, embrace the possibilities. Define your first principles. Dare to believe that the good in some is the good in all. And go out and change the world, with each act of compassion, rendered one day at a time."*

Prof. Juviler had office hours on Tuesdays from 2–4pm, but with the line outside his office sometimes extending all the way down the hall, those would last often until 6, 7 or 8pm. I would sit patiently, reviewing my notes, and I couldn't help but overhear the meticulous care and presence of mind that he brought to every single student who appeared at his doorstep. However long it took, Prof. Juviler sat, captivated and deeply interested, as if he had all the time in the world and what you had to say was ripe with the promise of true brilliance. This no matter the stack of correspondence that sat beside his typewriter, and the volumes of materials organized at his feet that were a part of his impressive scholarly agenda. When it was my turn, I would sometimes begin apologetically and say, *"Professor, you must be exhausted. We can reschedule."* He would hear none of it. *"No, no, no, I am so happy to see you."* And he was.

All these years later, as I sit for office hours, often with a line of students waiting, I find myself greeting each and every one with that same, *"I am so happy to see you."* And I am. When I get weary, I remind myself that this is the art and this is the point. Our students are the future's game-changers, paradigm- shifters and last best hope. As teachers we are fortunate beyond measure because we get to be a part of their path.

The generosity that I have observed from my best teachers is with me every time I encourage my classes to commit to compassionate service. The exemplars in my life are front-mind when I teach that wisdom and compassion are indivisible—one cannot be sustained without the other. Their integrity is there when I remember, on the battlegrounds of our adversarial system, that while kindness will sometimes be misunderstood as weakness, it can be expected only from the secure. Cruelty comes from fragility.

Your best teachers will expect great things from you, and you will rise to their level of expectation.

Good teachers understand that people rise and fall to meet our level of expectation of them. My finest teachers expected great things from me, even when their estimations of my promise exceeded my own. I rose to meet them because I could not bear to let them down. Seek out teachers like that. Look for the ones who refuse to respond to the naysayers (including your own voices of self-doubt) in kind. The best teachers implicitly embrace the wisdom that German philosopher Goethe rendered centuries ago: *If we treat people as they are, we make them worse. But if we treat people as they could be, we help them to become that.*

Carry your most treasured teachers in your heart.

Good teaching and good lawyering require mindfulness—the choice to be fully present in the moment. I remember hearing of the reminiscences of a monk who would make annual pilgrimages to the mountaintop, taking in the view and perspective from higher ground, only to then have to descend to work in the fields. When asked from the trenches to explain the point of those arduous climbs, he replied, *"So I can remember to carry the mountaintop in my heart."*

I have been a law professor and attorney for thirty years. For each one of those years I have carried my most treasured teachers in my heart. My time spent in the trenches has obliged me to find my own answer to the question, *"Who do you think you are?"* When I answer: *I am a crusader for social justice, I am a champion of the underdog, I am a voice for those who have yet to find their* own, I am a giver of hope, what I am really saying is, I am my best teachers' student.

Your best teachers can be living or historical, real or fictional.

Whose student are you? Your role models can be actual or fictional, living or historical. You can stand on the shoulders of the countless giants who have come before you. Some you know and some you know of. Think about the people or characters you admire most. Learn about them. Read about them. Then take them into your heart and carry them with you. When I write scholarly articles, I think of the elegance of the great jurists whose words were majestic and moving. When I prepare for the adversarial process, I embrace the integrity and passion of the great trial lawyers of history and literature. In negotiations, I imagine the statesmanship of our greatest diplomats.

We are neurologically equipped to mirror the examples of our best teachers.

We are hard-wired to readily emulate what others do. Neuroscientists describe the work of our mirror neurons, which allow us to empathize, feel and make real the experiences of others. Think of how you salivate when watching another bite into a delicious meal. Recollect the joy you felt when watching a contestant win the million-dollar prize, or the tension in your legs as you watched a tightrope artist walk on the wire. Those are your mirror neurons at work, the same tool chest that can enable you to simulate the best practices of others.

PART 4

How to Assure Your Success and Significance in Law School, at Work and in Life

In this section you will find a series of "how-to" best practices to habituate and make your own. They will assure your success and most essentially your significance throughout your law school and legal career and beyond. Turn to each of these chapters depending on the day and the circumstance at hand.

CHAPTER 17

How to Begin Each Day

Start each day with two words: *Thank you.*

As soon as you wake up, say thank you because you did wake up. You are still here. This day is a new beginning, a fresh start, another opportunity to say what needs to be said and to do what needs to be done. This is your day to make life easier for someone else. Say thank you for that privilege.

Say thank you because you have something to do and somewhere to be. Say thank you because there is a roof over your head. Spend some time in a homeless intake center to know the despair that comes when one is without a place in this world. Say thank you because you have a good mind and a good heart. Say thank you because you have family and friends who love you.

Say thank you because you will have something to eat today. Say thank you because you will have a means of transportation. Say thank you, thank you, thank you because you have a purpose that is mighty and you are on an elite career path. Say thank you to the countless clients and constituencies, most still nameless and unknown to you, who are waiting for you to finish school so that you can make their lives better.

Say thank you for all the good to come. Dwell on the promise of this day. You will find that a grateful heart does not have much room for the lesser instincts.

Be guided by your heroes.

On your bathroom mirror and on your refrigerator door keep pictures of the legal greats whose examples inspire you most. On post-its throughout your home or apartment, keep words that remind you of the promise of this world and your place in it. Our minds are constantly processing messages consciously and subconsciously. Feed your mind with words and examples of hope and aspiration.

On my bulletin board I keep the words of Dr. Martin Luther King, Jr., *"Injustice anywhere is a threat to justice everywhere."* On my laptop, I have an excerpt of President Franklin Delano Roosevelt's second inaugural address: *"Governments make mistakes. So do presidents. But the immortal Dante tells us that heaven weighs the sins of the cold-blooded and the warm-hearted on two very different scales. Let it be said that our mistakes are made in the name of compassion. Let it never be said that we have become frozen in the ice of our own indifference."*

To help my children to stay on purpose, I keep index cards with powerful messages in their sights. On my son's bedroom wall there is Booker T. Washington's wisdom, *"Let no one pull you so low as to make you hate them."* My daughter keeps *"Kindness Matters"* on her keychain.

As you step out the door, indicate your willingness to be delighted by this day.

As you leave the house, ask to be found precisely where you need to be. State your willingness to be the face of compassion for another. Indicate your readiness to be inspired by this day. Declare that you are going to seek and find the good in others. Ask to be used for a purpose mightier than yourself. If you are short for time, simply send up the quick prayer, *"Find me where you need me to be."* Stated even more succinctly, say *"Use me."*

How to Take the Advice of Others

The Economic Value of a Law Degree

The business of legal education, law school and the decision to become a lawyer has inspired a tremendous amount of conversation lately. Some of it has been negative, and many of those assessments have been lop-sided and less than fully informed. First, with respect to the criticism that the law degree "simply isn't worth it," I commend to your attention the fine work by my colleague, Prof. Michael Simkovic and Frank McIntyre on *The Economic Value of a Law Degree* (2013) available at http://papers.ssrn.com/sol3/papers.cfm?abstract_id=2250585. In this careful empirical analysis, the authors demonstrate that a law degree provides a large boost to earnings that is worth about $1,000,000 at the mean and $600,000 at the median. After you take out taxes and tuition, a law degree remains a very profitable investment.

Stay true to the study methods that have served you well in the past.

Second, setting aside the advice that you are apt to receive on the financial side of things, you will also find (if you haven't already) that just about everyone, from friends to colleagues to distant relatives, will have lots of advice on how to survive law school. You are likely to be laden with a host of tips, pointers, suggestions and shortcuts. **Take the advice of others with a big grain of salt.** Yes, law school will expose you to a new way of thinking and approaching problems. But the fundamental skills that got you here remain the same. Stay true to the study methods that have served you well in the past.

Ask your professors for guidance on how to approach and summarize the material.

For guidance on how best to approach your studies, talk to your professors. Each of us is best-situated to share with you our expectations, what we value most on an exam, and how to assimilate the subject matter that we teach. Ask your professors for their recommendations on former students who might be good resources. Then turn to those students who were in the class that you are now taking, who had the same teacher that you now have and who did well in the course. They will be a terrific help.

The voice in your head telling you that you cannot do this is a liar.

Law school can be very good at fostering self-doubt. Even the most competent people will sometimes feel inadequate or stupid. Especially at those times, try hard to remember who you are and all that you have already achieved. That voice in your head trying to convince you that you are "less than" is a liar.

Being lost at times is part of the process.

To avoid doubting yourself, seek positive regard from those who know you and, in particular, those who love you. Parents can be very helpful in this context, as can other family members, partners, close friends and old roommates. Call a friend from college and say, *"Tell me again about the time I aced that really tough Economics exam,"* or, *"Remember when I got that A in Philosophy. Let's talk about that."*

To keep your spirits up, it is important that you periodically reach out to the people who are best at helping you to maintain your sense of self and your capabilities. Risk being vulnerable and ask someone who cares about you, *"Am I stupid? How come I'm not getting it?"* Surround yourself with people who will reply, loudly:

"YOU ARE SMART AND TALENTED AND HARD-WORKING AND YOU ARE MAKING SOMETHING OUT OF YOUR LIFE AND WE ARE PROUD OF YOU AND WE WISH WE COULD BE YOU! KEEP AT IT BECAUSE YES YOU CAN DO THIS AND YES YOU WILL DO THIS!"

Proclaim those words about yourself every day. They tell the truth about you.

CHAPTER 19

How to Settle Down to Hard Work

"Forget about the likes and dislikes and do what must be done."

To settle down to hard work, *settle down and work hard*. This is not rocket science. It is not about which subjects you like and which you don't like. It is not about whether or not you are happy in this moment as you are stuck in the library while your friends are out having fun. George Bernard Shaw said it best, *"Forget about the likes and the dislikes and do what must be done. For now, this is not about happiness. This is about greatness.*

The rewards will come.

Put away your desire for immediate gratification, control your impulses to want to go to the refrigerator every six minutes or check game scores or tap into social media *and do what must be done*. The short-term sacrifice will yield long-term gains. I promise you that. In law school and in the practice, I spent countless evenings and weekends studying while my friends partied. When I started to feel resentful, I reminded myself that I was on a track to glory, that to finish this race would be to win the race, and that the rewards would come. They did. I am grateful for a career even more meaningful than I could have imagined. Stay on track and stay on purpose. *The rewards will come.*

Buy your ticket.

Do not be afraid to work hard. There is no secret mystery to succeeding in law school or in the practice. In law school, while some of the terminology and methodology will be different, the study skills are the same capabilities that you already possess and know how to apply: reading, writing and critical thinking. The key ingredient now is hard work. That is your ticket.

There is the old joke about the man who prays every day, *"Dear God, please let me win the lottery."* Day after day, failing to win, he sends up the same prayer. Finally, angry and frustrated, he yells at God, *"Why haven't I won yet?"* By this time, God has had enough. He answers, *"Listen, I can grant your request, but first you have to buy a ticket!"*

Buy your ticket now. Resolve that you will put in the time, dedication and energy that your studies and professional endeavors require. There are no short cuts and no substitutes for that investment of time. For that matter, you would not want short cuts. The stakes are too high. In law school, you are studying not just for the sake of an exam. You are learning for the purpose of applying that knowledge to your life's work. In the practice, people are depending on you to make the difference that only you can make.

Your work is your character made visible to others. You want the esteem in which you are held to reflect your highest

and best qualities. The people who matter in your life can't see what you won't show them. Do your best. Show your best.

Set aside blocks of time to do your work.

Set aside big blocks of time, sit at a desk with your books and laptop, and do the work that needs to be done. In school, think about the assigned readings. Put them into context, using your casebook's table of contents as your guide. Talk to your classmates about the material. Talk with your professor about the material. Turn to a study aid or hornbook when you need to. As a practitioner, give 100% to each effort. Edit, redraft and keep working at your craft. Feel immense pride in your work product.

Keep your daily study habits uncluttered.

To habituate good study and work habits, keep it simple. Do not clutter your day with too many to-do lists. Mariano Rivera, the dazzling Yankees' relief pitcher and the stuff of baseball legend, described what he does this way: *"I get the ball, I throw the ball, and then I take a shower."* Similarly, keep your daily practice unencumbered by distraction.

In other words: *In school, get the book and read the book. In practice, do the work. Review the work. Then take a shower.*

CHAPTER 20

How to Create Value

Add to your stock of social capital.

Be sure to create value every day. You create value when you add to your stock of social capital by making friends, networking and giving of your time and resources to help others. Be generous for your sake. Your commitment to the good of others will bring good to you. It is what Alexis DE Tocqueville called "self-interest rightly understood." Do for others with the confidence that they will gladly reciprocate. **We assure our success when we help others attain theirs.**

Remember that you are no longer studying simply for an exam and no longer working solely for your own advancement.

You create value when you remain mindful of the essential truth that you are no longer studying simply for an exam or practicing solely for your own promotion. You are studying for life and working for the good of others. Everything that you are learning in law school will have a place in your professional labors. Even if you think you know which area of law will be yours, all areas of law will present themselves throughout the trajectory of your long and brilliant career. Treat each course as if your career depended on it. It very well may.

In the workforce, remember that you are serving for purposes that transcend your own. You are working so that justice can be made visible. No matter the pretext (*"I am a prosecutor," "I am a transactional attorney," "I am a litigator," "I am a public defender"*), your job is to be a giver of hope. You are doing what you do to show others the face of compassionate discernment and the promise of the rule of law, so that everyone who is fortunate enough to be in your midst might come to know that while *"compassion without technique is a mess, technique without compassion is a menace."* Your fusion of generosity and rigor will change the world for the better.

Your classmates and co-workers are your colleagues. Treat them with respect.

As you look around your classes and place of work, know that the people in your midst are not only friends, classmates or co-workers. They are your colleagues. They are and will continue to be an integral part of your professional development and future success. Never lose sight of that. You will be counting on them and them on you for many years to come. Treat everyone with respect and kindness. Build bridges. Refrain from making snap judgments or speaking ill of anyone.

The legal community is smaller and even more inter-connected than you might think. People's memories are long. You want to be thought of and talked about as a person of great integrity and commitment to excellence. You want people to think of you as a good and generous person.

Hear me now and believe me later: The impression that you make on your classmates and colleagues will follow you into perpetuity. In the years ahead, it will have the potential to help you or hurt you. Early on in practice, I needed to adjourn a deposition. Much to my relief, one of the attorneys for our adversary happened to be one of my law school classmates with whom I had always enjoyed a good rapport. I phoned him, and he graciously accommodated the request. Years later, at a conference where I was demonstrating my pedagogical techniques, an attendee stood and generously said, *"I was Paula's classmate in law school, and I am here to tell you that the kindness you see now was the same care that she showed back then."* How you treat every single person in your midst matters. It will return to you.

Create value in class and at work by being present and being prepared.

Treat your professors, colleagues and adversaries with respect. Show them by your demeanor that you are interested and committed to the task at hand and that you are a good faith player. Be an active listener. Make eye contact and do not hesitate to nod when you are getting the point and to politely speak up when you aren't.

Your teachers, classmates, colleagues and employers see much more than you think. They can tell when they have helped you to make a connection and when you are lost. They can read your nonverbal cues and they will catch any bit of attitude that you are throwing. They can very quickly discern when you have left the matter at hand to check on a score, social media site or the sale of the week. Not only will they perceive those digressions as disrespectful, but they will also lose some of their estimation of you. What is more, your online digressions are likely to be a distraction to those who can't help but see what is on your computer screen.

Your attitude matters. Everything that you say and do helps you to either create or lose value. I cannot begin to count the number of times that I have been asked to share my estimations of one of my current or former students, whether at a bench or bar function, a conference or even at a ball game or on the train. Those encounters, often unexpected and quite informal, speak volumes about how important it is that you make a good and meaningful impression. Be the most diligent person in every classroom. Be the most grateful and generous student, classmate, colleague and friend.

Be **what you would want said about you.**

CHAPTER 21

How to Read Your Casebook

The Case Method

The pedagogical approach used in law school is built around the case method. First introduced at Harvard Law School in 1870, the case method is designed to accustom the student to view the law not merely as a series of cut and dry rules but as a living, fluid, always evolving "seamless web." There are three essential elements of the case method: 1) the casebook, 2) a final exam that consists of several "hypotheticals" or fact patterns and 3) active classroom discussion.

Using your casebook

You will be assigned a casebook for each of your classes. Each casebook contains a series of cases that set forth legal principles that have progressed over time to meet changing facts and circumstances. Organized according to topic, each case is usually followed by a set of interesting questions and comments aimed at heightening your understanding of the subject matter and eliciting further thought.

The casebook is used as the principal means to teach and learn the law because case law (the product of judicial opinions) is not fixed or immutable. It is not etched in stone. Instead, it is fluid and responsive to the particular facts and circumstances of the controversy at hand. Cases issue rulings (called holdings) to resolve the matter before the court, and court opinions usually also contain *dicta,* or relevant asides that might help to predict future outcomes based on different facts.

Use your casebook's table of contents as the roadmap for each course. Refer to it often. It will reveal to you where the material will take you and the class. As you read each case, know that it is telling you a story. Your job is to be able to re-tell that story, understanding its moral and its essential takeaways.

Recollect your time as an undergraduate or even as a high school student in an English class. Sometimes you would be assigned a short story or poem and asked to re-tell it, paying attention to its more noteworthy elements. Reading a case involves the same analytical process, in a different context.

At first, the cases may strike you the way that your first reading of Shakespeare or *The Canterbury Tales* struck you. You might not have a clue about what is going on. But you figured out Hamlet and you came to understand Chaucer. Maybe you needed Spark Notes to give you a sense of the forest and some of its trees, and maybe now you will need a study aid to do the same, but ultimately you made and will continue to make the material your own. You will get it. Be patient.

At first, you may be frustrated by the case method for learning the law. That frustration is understandable and it will pass.

Initially, your casebooks can be a source of frustration. They are very different from college and graduate school textbooks because they contain very little narrative. Instead, they allow the cases themselves to do the talking, and ask that you extract relevant doctrine from the text of the judicial opinions themselves only to then modify that doctrine on the basis of later rulings. This is all by design, to accustom you to the life of the law and its attendant uncertainties. As noted, use the casebook's table of contents as your roadmap and as a way to organize the cases according to topic and subheading. Refer to it often to remind you of where the material has been, where it is now, and where it is headed. Build your own outline of the assigned readings by using the table of contents as your guide.

Within a few weeks of patient commitment to the task of reading cases, you will get much better at it and much more efficient too. Put in the time now, however long it takes, to read and re-read the assigned materials. For the first month of law school, it would sometimes take me one hour just to get through and come to some understanding of one case. The task was torture at first, but it was worth it. Soon, like someone who gets on a treadmill for the first time but sticks with it day after day, I was able to go from a crawl to a decent jog. Keep at it, day in and day out, and it will get easier and you will get stronger.

"It depends."

A common answer to any question posed in class as the cases are presented and discussed will be, "*It depends.*" It depends on the particular facts that yielded the controversy. It depends on the jurisdiction. It depends on the nuances of the precedent. It depends on the court's composition.

Relish the uncertainties. If the law was fixed and immutable, justice would be disserved and there would be no need for lawyers. A *"one size fits all"* conceptualization of justice seldom achieves justice. The law's capacity to change based on the particular case before the court and evolving sensibilities remains a saving grace.

Your hard work will pay off.

Endure the initial frustration and trust that your hard work is worth it and will be rewarded. Careful casebook reading now will prepare you for the challenges of law practice. As a lawyer, you will be researching and then reading judicial precedent—the case law—to learn not only what the law is but how new and different facts might be wielded to alter the law. Each of the clients and causes that you take up will present facts that are similar to but also different from the weight of precedent. As a lawyer, you will have the privilege to advance the cause of justice by using the law's fluidity to alter for the better the flow of progress.

Indeed, no matter where your professional path takes you, whether as attorney, mediator, journalist, political officeholder, diplomat, corporate leader, social activist and the list goes on, you will need to know how to read cases. Think about some of the seminal cases announced just recently. Those trained in the art of the case method become interpreters for the world.

CHAPTER 22

How to Be Prepared for Class

When and how to brief the cases

Early on in law school, you will be taught how to brief a case. A brief is simply a summary, organized into headings according to the facts of the case, the issue presented to the court, the holding or rule of law announced by the court and your analysis of the court's decision. The task of briefing cases is time-consuming and it can be tedious, but do it regularly for the first few weeks of your first semester. Do it because the process teaches you how to read a case, and knowing how to read a case is essential to your life's work.

The court's opinion will help you to write your brief. The opinion will give you cues by inserting prefatory clauses such as, *"The issue before this court is _____"* (here comes the issue), *"The rule of law that we announce today _____"* (there is the holding), *"The case before us is distinguishable from earlier cases that _____"* (here is the analysis). Pay attention to the concurring opinions (a concurring opinion agrees with the majority's conclusion, but sets forth a different basis or rationale for adopting that conclusion) and dissenting opinions (the dissent disagrees with the majority's ruling, for reasons that it specifies).

Your brief is telling the story of the case. You can use plain language, and you can use your own shorthand, as long as you know what your words are referring you to. Include in your brief any questions about the case that you would like to raise in class and any problems or disagreement that you might have with the court's ruling or analysis.

After a few weeks of practice spent briefing cases, it will take you much less time to read cases. You will not need to commit to a formal briefing process for each case. Instead, take notes in your notebook, laptop and in the given casebook's margins. Those notes are important, because chances are that you will be called on in class, even when you do not raise your hand.

The Socratic Method

Most of your professors will employ some version of the Socratic Method. Named after the exchanges between Plato and his teacher, Socrates, the Socratic Method as traditionally practiced has the teacher asking a series of deliberate and careful questions of the student, so ordered as to help the student to arrive at an answer or conclusion. Today, many teachers use a modified version of that format, combining questions and answers with lectures on the points presented.

Whether practiced strictly or less traditionally, know that you will be called on in class. To help you to handle yourself under that pressure, be sure that the notes that you took on the material are legible and readily accessible. A few minutes before class, sit quietly and review your notes to refresh your recollection. That way, you will have something to say when you hear your name called.

When you do get called on, be thankful, because you have been given an opportunity to practice in a safe lab of sorts, your classroom. You have the benefit of a terrific coach, your teacher, and you have been given the chance to take practice swings that can only improve your game.

Bring talking points to each class.

Reading the cases, and taking careful notes, will help you to be well-prepared for class. In your notes, jot down a few talking points, or questions and comments that you would like to bring up during the class discussion. I actually began that practice in college, and continued it throughout law school. I would always try to assert at least one of those talking points, for several reasons. First, by forcing myself into the dialogue, I was able to practice speaking the language of the law. There is a certain methodology to the legal method of inquiry, and by repeatedly entering the fray to articulate a point or ask a question, I was becoming conversant in its lexicon. Second, jotting down talking points in advance of class prompted me to read more critically and more actively. I had to pay extra attention to the materials, to the extent that my professor asked follow-up questions.

If you are not prepared for class, send your professor an e-mail or leave a note at the podium.

Sometimes you will not be prepared for class. When that is the case, let your professor know in advance. Leave a note at the podium just before class begins. That is the best way to be sure that your teacher has received the message and it is more reliable than e-mail or voicemail. Letting your professor know that you are simply not up to being called on will relieve you (and everyone else) of the awkwardness of that moment when, in front of the entire group, you would have to say, "*I didn't get to the reading.*"

CHAPTER 23

How to Be in Class

Know that your professors see you.

Whether you are seated in a class of 100 or in a seminar of 15, your professor sees you. We see when you are engaged and attentive and when you have tuned out. We see when you have chosen to digress to do something on your laptop or phone that is not related to class discussion. We see when you are whispering to your neighbor or rolling your eyes. We see your yawns and we see your smiles.

Let your body language reflect that you are actively engaged. Sit upright. Make eye contact with the teacher. Nod when you understand the point. Listen intently and when you participate reference what the professor or a classmate said that is relevant to your point. If you disagree with someone or something, state so, but always in a generous and gracious way. When you are referring to a classmate in class, use the classmate's name rather than pronouns such as *"what s/he just said raises the problem that I too perceived."* Avoid all colloquialisms and be professional and respectful in your tone.

You are creating value (or not) with everything that you do (or fail to do) in class.

You want your professors and classmates to see and to think the very best of you. You do that when you adopt a respectful and kind demeanor. You do that when you are prepared. You do that when you are an active listener.

Liken each class to a court appearance. How do you want to be perceived? What are you hoping to achieve? You want to be perceived as an impeccable student and diligent soon to be professional. You want to create value and add to your stock of social and professional capital. You want your professors to think highly of you, so that when they are asked about you (and they will be asked about you, whether by prospective employers, colleagues, judges or the Character and Fitness Committee of the bar), they will speak only good of you.

In class, do not use your laptop for anything other than class purposes.

One of the surest ways to fall in your professor and classmates' estimations is to use your laptop in class for something other than class purposes. You will lose respect and inspire resentment. Be aware that any outside activities that you engage in are a distraction to those seated near you. That is unfair to your classmates. Remember too that your teacher sees you. Your digressions cast you as selfish, indifferent and cavalier, and that is not who or what you are.

Be a good classmate.

Dissuade your neighbor from digressing on his laptop. If he gets called on and needs some help, try to help. Point to where in the book he needs to be. When a classmate makes a good point, try to say so in class by weaving that point into your own contribution to discussion. After class, compliment that classmate, reiterating what a great job he or she did.

When a classmate needs the notes, be forthcoming. If a classmate is sick for more than a day or so, reach out and extend support. Offer your notes. Ask what else you might do to help.

If a classmate seems down, be particularly kind. When a classmate has reason to celebrate, share in his or her joy. When you think a good thought about a classmate, say it out loud. Be the most enthusiastic person in your class. Remember classmates' birthdays. Celebrate them. Honor special occasions.

Stir the pot of compassion and camaraderie everywhere you go. Be the most grateful person in every room. Seek out the good in every single person in your class. Expect to find it and you will.

Be the humanity that you want to see in class.

Infuse class discussion with your idealism and generosity. Our profession's future depends on nurturing and sustaining the essential goodness that you and your classmates possess. Be firm in your commitment to think about the people behind the cases that you read.

As you participate in class remind others of the humanity and humanness of the given subject matter at hand. Put people first. Consider the welfare of the parties before the court. Think about their likely struggles and the sorrows that resulted in the case before you. Most often, there are no true winners in litigation. There are only survivors. Was this lawsuit worth it? Was justice achieved? Is the court's decision imbued with the force of rightness?

Both in and out of class remember to honor your own humanness and fallibility. When you risk being vulnerable by revealing some of your own struggles and imperfections, you give others permission to do the same.

Be a leader of your class.

Organize efforts that will allow you and your classmates to celebrate the wins and commiserate when the load is heavy. Have bagel Fridays, remember each other's birthdays and milestones, surprise your professor with the snack or beverage that he or she seems to like and place it at the podium, find local places that are fun and get the class together there on a regular basis. Organize trips to volunteer at the local soup kitchen. Collect toys for the underprivileged. Cook or bake for a classmate who is sick. *Be the compassion that you want to see*.

How to Use the Language of the Law to Shine in Class

Seek out the words and phrases that inspire you and then use them.

As lawyers, our word is everything and our words matter. You want to begin building a fluency in the language of the law while enhancing your vocabulary. To help with that, keep a stack of index cards with you. On those cards, jot down words, phrases and quotes from the assigned readings that you thought particularly stirring. When your professor uses a turn of phrase that you like, write it down. Buy a small box to house your index cards, and look at them often. Incorporate the words that they contain in your daily exchanges and particularly when you participate in class.

The language of the law can be majestic.

Begin to think about which judge or justice's writing style you admire most. Seek to emulate his or her example in your own writing. As you sit down to complete a legal writing assignment or, later, draft a brief or memo, invoke that jurist's wisdom and let it infuse your work.

Words we love

In my classes, we keep a running list of words we love. Each semester, I assign a student to be the scribe or keeper of the words, and each time someone uses a word or phrase that makes the point efficiently but also beautifully, we add that word or phrase to the list. At the end of the semester, each class member receives a copy of the list.

If you think that your professor and class might enjoy an exercise like that, suggest it. Otherwise, keep your own running list of words you love. Turn to them often and practice using them.

Here are just a few of the very helpful words to build into your growing law-related vocabulary. Incorporate them readily.

- *Apposite* (not opposite). To be apposite is to be relevant or germane (not Janet or LaToya) to the matter at hand. For example, *"Your Honor, that case is entirely apposite here. Its precedent presents a blueprint for how best to analyze this matter."*

- *Inapposite* is the opposite of apposite. To be inapposite is to be irrelevant to the present matters. For example, *"Respectfully, Your Honor, the case that plaintiff cites is simply inapposite. There, the plaintiff sought money damages. Here, plaintiff is seeking injunctive relief."*

- *Draconian*. A rule or result that is draconian is unduly harsh and unreasonable. Named for the notorious Emperor Draco, a draconian rule is fixed and immutable. It tends to be devoid of a moral referent. Draconian results are to be avoided. For example, *"Your Honor, the mandatory sentencing guidelines are impossibly draconian. How can it be that my client is subject to incarceration for thirty years as a result of this petty first offense?"*

- **Salutary.** To be salutary is to be beneficial. For example, *"Your Honor, remanding this matter will achieve several salutary ends. It will afford the parties the opportunity to consider a settlement while also avoiding the added expenses of further appeal."*

- **Invites the question.** To invite a question is to present the given question with an eye toward answering it. For example, *"Your Honor, plaintiff has asserted that his car skidded because the road was wet. That invites the question of whether or not it was raining on the day of the accident."*

- **Begs the question.** Do not confuse *invites the question* with *begs the question*. To beg the question is to endeavor to avoid answering it (as in begging off the question.) Countless commentators misuse the phrase *begs the question*. Commit to its correct usage, and teach others to do the same. You beg the question when you try to escape providing a reply. For example, a colleague asks, *"Did you get the memo done?"* You reply, *"How about those Mets!"* You have just begged the question.

CHAPTER 25

What to Do When You Get Called On But Do Not Have the Answer

"To honor reasonable expectations"

Sometimes you will be caught off guard in class, and other times you will simply be stumped. When that happens, do not hesitate to say so. You are human and that is a good thing.

If you feel obliged to say something during those moments when you really do not have much to say, try these four words: *to honor reasonable expectations*.

When I was a law student, those four words came to me in my Tax class. I was called on to indicate why the Internal Revenue Code would afford a deduction for charitable gifts. As soon as I heard my name called, I jumped to attention to such an extent that I actually fell out of my chair. (Yes, sad but true. To this day my right knee bothers me because of that.) It is interesting that the professor continued to wait for my response, no matter that I was quite literally on bended knee. While still there, I blurted out, *"To honor reasonable expectations."* I could not think of anything

129

else to say. To my relief, the professor replied, *"Excellent!"* and continued on with the lecture. I then limped to the infirmary.

The law aims in all that it does to vindicate interests of certainty, reliability and predictability. It endeavors to be perceived as fair and just. In other words, the law seeks to honor reasonable expectations. Thus, for example, when you are asked why you think the court ruled as it did, or why the rule of law is as it is, or why the court abided precedent or, essentially, why any given result is just, simply answer, *"To honor reasonable expectations."* (Then, if you really are not too well-prepared, hope that there is no follow-up question. If there is, punt and say, *"I need to revisit my notes and think about that."*)

CHAPTER 26

How to Present a Case, an Oral Argument or a Speech

Prepare carefully.

Think of each presentation that you make as story-telling. Your job is to be the story-teller. Almost as a journalist would report on an event or an issue, your mission is to communicate *who, what, when, where and why*.

Take notes on the points that you would like to make. Then distill those notes down to several key points. Number them (aiming to have between three and five points that you plan to make.) Put those points on index cards or on a page in your notebook. Memorize those key points.

How to present the case, oral argument or speech

In advance, you will have with you your index cards of key points and you will have memorized those points. When the time comes to present, **put the cards down.** Indicate to your audience (whether it is the professor, a panel of judges, a jury or any other group) that you have three (or four or five) essential points to make. That will add an order to your presentation and it will keep the listener's attention as he or she waits for the points to advance.

When you get interrupted, answer the question presented. Do not say, *"I will get to that later."* That sort of response is disrespectful and ineffective, because the questioner wants his or her question answered now. If you delay answering, you will lose the questioner until you do address his or her inquiry. Once you have addressed the question presented, return to your talking points.

Do not be wedded to a script when you present an oral argument or make a speech.

Dr. Martin Luther King's historic 1963 speech on the mall in Washington, D.C. had been carefully scripted. It was only when Mahalia Jackson, a dear friend of the Reverend's, began yelling from the choir, *"Martin, tell them about the dream!"* that Dr. King ventured off script to speak to the great vision that became a cherished part of our nation's history.

Prepare a script but do not be wedded to it. When you are beholden to a script you are no longer in the moment. You want to be carefully prepared but also fully present. That way, you can be spontaneous and reactive when the opportunity strikes. When you are in the present moment, you are also more likely to make a connection that deserves mention and to know when to give a particular point added attention or less emphasis.

Once you have crafted your remarks, summarize them in three to five headings. Put buzz words under each of those headings to remind you of the topics or points that you plan to cover. Place the headings and catch phrases on an index card or single sheet of paper and place that sheet or card at the very top of your script. As you move through your remarks, slide it to the side of your script and use it to give you cues and also potentially free you from having to read from the script. In time, with practice and experience, you will be able to bring to the podium only that index card or single sheet of paper with your summary points.

Be responsive to the verbal and nonverbal cues of your audience.

At all times during your presentation, you need your wits about you and your emotional intelligence fully functioning. You want to be responsive to the verbal and nonverbal cues of your audience. Are the intended listeners listening, or do they seem distracted or restless? When the latter seems to be the case, be brave enough to switch course. With practice, you will soon be able to respectfully make statements like, *"I may have lost Your Honor's attention. If it pleases the court, please allow me to state the matter somewhat differently,"* or, *"It seems that it might be more effective for me to move away from this point and onto the next."*

Honor the art in you, and not you in the art.

Leave your ego at the door. That way, you become less self-conscious because once you leave your ego out of it, the presentation is no longer about you. It is about telling a story that is anchored in the pursuit of justice. It is about touching the minds and hearts of the listeners. It is about leaving the room better than when you entered, because you were there.

Whether you shine or flop does not matter. What matters is that your intent was noble and that you learned from the experience. You will be even better next time. Keep at it. Repetition is the parent of mastery.

CHAPTER 27

What to Do in Classes That Leave You Uninspired

If you are feeling alienated or lost in some classes, speak up.

Sometimes, the value of good teaching is not emphasized enough in law school. If you are feeling uninspired or confused in some classes, speak up and recognize that you are no doubt not alone. Sometimes the Socratic Method, when practiced strictly, can be frustrating. Based on the ancient dialogues between Socrates and his student, Plato, it may work well when two engaged philosopher-kings are sitting alone on a rock, but it tends to lose some of its effectiveness when practiced before a large group.

First, with so many listening, the student on the hot seat cannot help but feel nervous and self-conscious. That anxiety is an impediment to the very sort of connection-making that the Socratic Method is supposed to inspire. Cognitive psychology and, increasingly, neuroscience make plain that performance is

135

enhanced immeasurably by calm. It is hard to remain calm when a room full of classmates and a learned professor are scrutinizing your responses to questions that eventually make a point but in the moment seem to be coming from left field. When you see a classmate squirming, go to his or her rescue. Raise your hand, and respectfully articulate as best as you can the confusion that he (and most likely the rest of the class) is experiencing.

Second, when used dispassionately, the Socratic Method can do little to foster a sense of how the attributes of justice, virtue and compassion can and should be relevant both in evaluating case law and then putting precedent into practice. Sometimes it will feel as though the people and very human problems behind the cases remain there, with moral concerns and considerations of basic decency yielding to abstractions. When it seems that the classroom exchange is devoid of a moral referent, raise your hand and say so.

Third, in the wrong hands, the Socratic Method becomes a basis for games of one-upmanship, where the learned professor demonstrates his prowess at the game using the student, a novice, as his foil. That is unfair, unbecoming and inappropriate. At its worst, it produces a classroom atmosphere that is cold, impersonal and maybe even contentious. Sometimes it will bring out the lesser virtues of some of your classmates as they emulate the teacher's example. When that happens, *rather than be the thermometer, be the thermostat*. Bring warmth into the room by raising your hand and introducing the voice of reasoned compassion into the mix.

Thankfully, law teaching has evolved so that many law teachers today are in fact excellent teachers, who use a modified version of the Socratic Method or their own pedagogical techniques to actually teach the material and inspire their students to engage in critical discussion. You will have some outstanding teachers who value the experiential and more accessibly meaningful dimensions of the given topic, no matter what the subject matter happens to be. They will remind you that the material ultimately is about the people, societal issues and policy concerns behind the cases and statutory text. Your best teachers will help you to understand not only what the law is *but what it means* in very real settings.

Raise your hand and make your point. Do not let the tenor of any classroom experience silence you or cause you to be complicit in the silencing of another.

When you feel disconnected from the material, uninspired or disaffected in class, have the courage to raise your hand and speak up. Make your point respectfully and back it up by your careful reading of the assigned materials, but **do make your point.** Do not allow any classroom exchange to make you feel small or cause you to be complicit in the silencing of another.

Be clear about your intent before you raise your hand in class. Set as your intent the desire to add to the caliber of discussion in an intellectually honest and principled way. Do not raise your hand simply to show off or cause harm.

Your intention is the single most important thing that you bring to any context. Make sure that your intent is to be a virtuous contributor. Have you raised your hand to show off or to show up the teacher or a classmate? Then put your hand down. Have you raised your hand to make a principled point, add clarification, seek clarification, facilitate mutual understanding or introduce compassion and the moral referent? Then keep your hand up and speak up often. Remember that whatever you intend is what you yourself will reap. When your intent is virtuous, you will be perceived as such and you will reap virtue's rewards.

How to be a principled voice of reason and compassion in class

Here are some helpful and considerate ways to add meaning to class discussion, allay your frustrations and provide a conduit for enhanced exchange. Allow them to help you to arrive at a working lexicon within which to communicate your perceived shortcomings with the dynamic at hand or your own difficulties in contributing meaningfully.

- *"This case is telling the story of a group of people whose lives are forever changed for the worse because of the court's decision. How do we reconcile that with the aims of justice?"*

- *"It feels as though the court has divorced a sense of humanity from the resolution of the matter at hand. Here's my basis for that perception. Am I right, and, if so, how would we as lawyers remediate that deficiency?"*

- *"Judges and lawyers are not automatons or technicians. Like the litigants before them, they are people. It seems that the court's own biases may have affected the outcome here. Here's my intuition about that. Could I be right?"*

- *"We haven't talked yet about the ethical and moral issues implicated by this case or topic. Just because someone has a right to do something doesn't mean that it is the right thing to do. What would have been the right thing to do in this case? It seems to me that a better outcome could have been achieved, but I'm not sure how."*

- *"In listening to this exchange, I'm noticing that many of us (including me) find it hard to talk about these issues. Maybe that's because we haven't yet found a way to articulate our thoughts without potentially causing offense or risking being misunderstood. Can you help us to develop a helpful vocabulary and skill set to talk about these emotionally-fraught issues?"* (This sort of concern is very relevant in classes that get to issues of bias, discrimination and more charged socio-political issues.)

- *"I understand the rule, but how does it apply in real life? How would we use it in our work as lawyers?"*

How to Survive Family Law Days

Family Law Days: When a Family Member or Friend of a Family Member Puts You on the Spot by Asking You a Legal Question

Participate in class often. (See the preceding chapters on how to do that well). Among its many benefits, getting into the habit of speaking in class will prepare you for the rigors of Family Law Days. Those days take their name not because they involve matters of family law (although they could), but because they involve a family member or friend of a family member who puts you on the spot by asking you a legal question, usually in the presence of a large crowd all of whom are anxious to learn whether this investment in your legal education is actually worth it.

Those potentially uncomfortable encounters may have already taken place for some of you, perhaps almost from the moment that you received your first acceptance to law school. For others, Family Law Day is an imminent reality, and typically occurs for the first time within weeks of your matriculating. It often happens on a Sunday, either at your parents' home or at some other forum where the potential for embarrassment is great. In fact, it tends to occur when you are caught totally off guard, wearing sweatpants and not yet showered. A family member, friend or friend of a friend you've never seen before but who knows your name just happens to be in the neighborhood and is wondering, since you are in law school, how she can sue for back child support payments, or how he might set up a tax shelter under the new tax regulations, or how she might incorporate her new business venture, and so on. The possibilities are vast and limitless.

Now, those are questions that you cannot possibly answer after a few weeks (let alone the first year) of law school. Unfortunately, lay people assume otherwise. But here is the good news. Because you have been speaking in class, you are at least already somewhat fluent in the language of the law—fluent enough that you can punt with credibility, thereby preserving your family's reputation in the community.

My First Family Law Day

My first Family Law Day took place at my parent's house, just before my first semester law school exams. My mother had asked me to check on the lasagna, and then was wondering why my head was in the oven for such a long time. Suddenly, a friend of one of our cousins just happened to be in the neighborhood and wanted to know from me what the capital gain tax consequences would be of his investments in municipal bonds. At this point, all activity in the household ceased. My parents, siblings, our neighbor Sadie and two people whose identities to this day remain unknown together with the family pet Alfonso intently stared at me, awaiting my response and eager to see how much I was learning in law school.

I had no clue as to the answer. But because I had been called on repeatedly in class, and had gotten into the habit of participating, I could hedge in an artful way, invoking with credibility the legal dialect. I responded, *"The answer to your question is, quite frankly, 'it depends.' It depends on the language of the statute as amended, recent judicial interpretations and, of course, the fact-specific nature of the transactions themselves. All of this would need to be fleshed out, explored and then reconciled."*

My parents beamed. My siblings clapped. My dad let me have the family car for the rest of the year. Speaking in class has its rewards.

CHAPTER 29

How to Make Penne Vodka

Now that you have survived Family Law Day, it is time to celebrate. Get your family, friends, classmates and colleagues together to cook. This chapter, while outside the province of the law, may come in handy to the extent that you wish to prepare a wonderful meal.

Later in his life, my dad became an acclaimed chef. In the 1970s at Orsini's Restaurant in New York City, he was asked to prepare a pasta dish tableside for two of the eating establishment's more esteemed patrons. My dad obliged the request, and began to create a sauce with a tomato and cream base. He needed to reduce the sauce just a bit. On a whim, he tossed his glass of vodka (inspiration that he kept nearby) into the mix. The sauce let off the most enticing aroma, immediately inspiring patrons to ask, *"Luigi, what are you preparing?"* My dad replied in a flash, *"Penne à la Russia, because of the addition of fine Russian vodka."* *Penne à la Russia* caught on quickly, and within a few years became a staple on Italian restaurant menus. In turn, my dad enjoyed his fifteen minutes of fame on the talk show circuit, where he prepared the dish to the delight of late-night viewers.

In its later iterations, the dish came to be known as *penne vodka*. This is the original recipe, as devised by my dad and told by my mom:

Ingredients:

- 1 stick butter

- 1 tbsp. olive oil

- 1 medium onion chopped

- 2 large cans of crushed tomatoes or tomato puree and 1 can of water

- 1 pint of heavy cream

- ½ cup vodka

- ¼ tsp. red crushed pepper

- ½ pound freshly grated parmesan cheese

Method:

- Melt butter and oil in heavy pan over medium heat. Add chopped onion and sauté until translucent (approximately 8 minutes). Stir throughout.

- Add tomatoes together with 1 can of water and cook on low heat for 25 minutes.

- Add heavy cream, vodka and red pepper. Add one handful of parmesan cheese to sauce and stir well.

- Boil until thickened (2 minutes).

- Only add salt after you taste the sauce, and then add salt to taste.

- Cook pasta *al dente* in large pot of water, adding salt and 1 tsp. olive oil to the water to prevent the pasta from sticking.

- Drain well. Pour sauce over pasta and toss well.

- Sprinkle with cheese.

CHAPTER 30

How to Be a Generous Classmate, Colleague and Friend

The key to being a good classmate, colleague and friend is reducible to two words: **Be generous.** Commit to the practices set forth below, for others' sake and for your sake too. In a world of infinite possibilities, you do not get what you want. *You get what you are.* A generous person lives in a generous world. A person who rejoices in another's achievements assures his own success.

What we think about most is what we move towards. Look for the excellence in your midst and seek to emulate it. Think about what you admire in others, and emulate that. Your life will move in the direction of your predominant thoughts. You can choose those thoughts. Choose to celebrate achievement, your own and others'. Choose to exalt in the many causes for hopefulness. Proclaim those loudly. The faultfinders seem so prevalent because they are so noisy. Move away from that cacophony of grievance and lead the team of cheerleaders for the good.

Be generous with your knowledge.

If a classmate gets called on and is struggling, subtly try to help, perhaps by pointing to the right spot in the casebook or whispering the answer. When I see this happening in my classes, I smile, because it tells me that my students are forming a community and building camaraderie. I want that collective spirit to be anchored in the truth that success in infinite and contagious. There is room at the top for everyone.

If a classmate asks for your notes, share them. If a classmate asks to see your outline, share it. If you uncover a great case that is helpful to a legal writing assignment, share it. Do not fall into the trap of believing that success is limited, and that yours can only be assured at the expense of others. That is nonsense. Moreover, the ultimate measure of your success and significance in law school and beyond will be the content of your character. You will be treasured and held in the highest esteem because you were kind and generous to your classmates. You endeavored to help when you could. You were a team player.

Be generous with your praise.

When a classmate, colleague or friend does well, be happy, truly happy, for him or her. Communicate that joy and be generous with your praise. Jealousy always backfires. It never hurts the other, but it always hurts you. Let others' success inspire you, not deflate you. Success is contagious. You get it by learning from and emulating the habits of successful people.

Moreover, by reveling in another's achievements, and thinking about and speaking about those accomplishments with great excitement, you are signaling that that is what you admire. Your life will move in the direction of what you admire when you keep your positive regard there. *Like attracts like.*

Be generous with your sphere of influence, opportunity and goodwill.

Perhaps you have a cousin who is a prosecutor, and a classmate whose life dream is to work in the prosecutor's office. Make the connection on behalf of your classmate. Maybe a friend in class is very interested in doing real estate work. Because you attended a networking reception, you met an attorney who not only does just that, but also invited you to observe an upcoming closing. Tell your friend about it and ask if he or she would like to attend the closing too.

In your travels, be interested in the people around you. Everyone has a story to tell and something to teach you.

You never know what the person sitting next to you on the train might mean to you or someone in your midst. I always strike up conversations on trains, planes, at airports and on long lines, with the hope that the person I meet might be able to help my students in some way. Time and again, that hope is realized. On a flight to Los Angeles I sat next to a filmmaker who I put in touch with one of my students interested in practicing entertainment law. On a train to Boston I met a practitioner based in Philadelphia who became a mentor to my student seeking to do employment law there. The list goes on. Here is the other unintended consequence of my making a habit of reaching out on others' behalf: my own life has been enriched in countless unexpected ways. By helping others grow in stature, my own success has been assured. There is a force that meets good with good.

You will grow in stature the more you help others grow in theirs.

Prof. Adam Grant, an organizational psychologist who teaches at the Wharton Business School, has engaged in considerable research and best practices that make plain that "giving is the secret to getting ahead." The New York Times Magazine recently reported on Prof. Grant's work this way:

> Scores of studies and personal case histories suggest the benefits of an attitude   of extreme giving at work. Many of the examples—the selfless C.E.O.'s, the consultants who mentor ceaselessly—are inspiring and humbling, even if they are a bit intimidating in their natural expansiveness. These generous professionals look at the world the way Grant does: an in-box filled with requests is not a task to be dispensed with perfunctorily (or worse, avoided); it's an opportunity to help people, and therefore it's an opportunity to feel good about yourself and your work. "I never get much done when I frame the 300 e-mails as 'answering e-mails,' " Grant told me. "I have to look at it as, How is this task going to benefit the recipient?" Where other people see hassle, he sees bargains, a little work for a lot of gain, including his own. ("Is Giving the Secret to Getting Ahead?" The New York Times Magazine, March 27, 2013).

By practicing altruism for its own sake, Prof. Grant has enhanced exponentially his own success. His generosity is reciprocated in countless, often unforeseeable ways. His research makes plain that what we do for others we do for ourselves.

Self-interest rightly understood

Be generous for your own sake. Systems of reciprocity (or "one hand washes the other") are always at work, and what you do for others will be returned to you in kind. The value that you create in law school, at work and in relationships will yield dividends for many years to come. Because you are held in high esteem, when a former classmate needs to make a referral on a matter outside his expertise but within yours, he will refer you. When another former classmate is sitting on the Judicial Appointments Committee and a judgeship opens up in your county, she will put your name up. When you need an adjournment on a matter and opposing counsel happens to be one of your former classmates, you will be more apt to get the time you need.

No matter how seemingly vast, the legal community is actually quite small, and everyone is within six degrees of separation from everyone else.

You want only good things said of you. As you ascend, whether running for office, receiving a Cabinet appointment, being vetted for a judgeship or being appointed Special Master of a complex litigation, the press and the fact-checkers will swoop in to learn more about you. They will interview your former professors, classmates and co-workers to gain a better measure of you. You will not be able to control who they choose to talk with. You want to create a record of achievement and character that renders you unassailable. You want good things said about the person you were, because that will inform the public's perception of the person you are.

CHAPTER 31

How to Be When You Are Outside of Class and Out of the Office

In the hallways, elevator and cafeteria

Make it a habit to make eye contact with everyone that you encounter. Smile at every person you see. Greet the security guard at the door with enthusiasm and joy because you are happy to be here today. If you do not feel particularly happy, fake it until you make it. Act like the most joyful person in the world, and watch what happens. You will be met at that level of expression, and soon have reasons to be glad.

Strike up conversations with everyone. Say hello to the people you know and those you do not yet know. Greet everyone on the staff. Acknowledge the hard work of the janitor who is cleaning the halls. Thank the postal carrier who comes in with the mail. Express your appreciation to the person who made your sandwich and thank the cashier who rings you up.

When you are thinking something complimentary about someone, say it out loud. For example, if you notice that another person in the elevator is dressed exceptionally well, say so. If you bump into a professor who just released a new book, congratulate him or her. It does not matter whether you formally know the given person to whom you are directing the compliment or not. Take as a given that you are all part of the same family in the law. Treat your *in-the-laws* with respect and appreciation. When you are thinking something kind about any one of them, get out of your self-consciousness and tell them.

In every context, see what needs to be seen. Notice when someone needs a hand, and then offer to help. Notice when a classmate seems down, and offer an encouraging word. Notice when the person emptying the waste baskets seems exhausted, and buy her a cup of coffee.

In restrooms

Do not say anything in a public restroom that you would not want repeated. Public restrooms are public, and while you are at the sink washing your hands and commiserating with a classmate, colleague or friend, chances are that someone is behind a stall. You do not know who that person is, and you do not want to compromise yourself or anyone else by saying something that is simply not worthy of you.

I was using a restroom in a restaurant in New York when two women came in and began speaking disparagingly about a colleague of theirs. I knew that colleague. At the sink I said, "*I know the person that you are referring to. I will not tell him anything of what I just heard, but the next person who overhears you could.*"

In public settings

In every public or quasi-public space on or off campus and your place of work, expect that everything that you say can and will be overheard. That rule applies when you are in school or at work, in the library, student center, café, restaurant, journal office or clinic. It applies when you are at an airport, train station, grocery store or shopping mall. Certainly, do not say anything that you would not want repeated. Be particularly mindful of this rule when you are on the phone.

Phone users submit to the delusion that only the person on the other end of the line can hear them. Remember that when you are on the phone, everyone around you can hear you. Exercise good judgment. Be quick and to the point until you can speak with the other privately. This will become even more important when you begin practicing. Whether on a train, plane or stuck in an airport, do not say anything to another that you would not want overheard by an adversary, a judge, a colleague, a reporter or anyone else. It is a small world, and you do not know who the person in the next seat or the next row could be.

At social occasions

As an attorney-in-training, you will soon be an officer of the court. As a lawyer, you are an officer of the court. Keep that in mind whenever you are in the public eye. In social settings, do not drink to excess. Do not become sloppy and end up saying things that you do not quite remember but still hope to forget. Certainly, NEVER DRINK AND DRIVE. A driving under the influence charge will hold up your admission to the bar and compromise your record with a blemish that you cannot afford.

On your way home from school or work

On the way to catch your train, do not rush past the homeless man or woman who needs a dollar. Give. At the traffic light, do not avoid making eye contact with the man begging for change. Give. There is likely to be a sea of need right outside your doorstep. Do not become desensitized to the suffering of others. Do what you can to help, whether in the form of a sandwich, a cup of coffee or some change or dollars that you have to spare.

"But," you might protest, *"He's only going to use the money to buy alcohol or drugs."* Maybe, but whatever he does with your donation is his business. *Your* business is choosing to give. You stir the pot of compassion every time you choose compassion over complacency. Your kindness will inspire others. You will be caught in the act of generosity and people will be called to follow your example. Every kind deed matters.

CHAPTER 32

How to Talk About
Your Day

Speak good things about your day.

When you are asked, *"How was your day?"* think before you issue a perfunctory response or launch into a litany of complaints. What you think about most and talk about most is what you move towards. To talk about what went wrong keeps you moving in that direction. You have the power to change course by choosing to think about, and talk about, what went right during the day. For example, *"I had a really great Contracts class today,"* or, *"I met such an interesting person on line in the cafeteria,"* or, *"I am the luckiest person on earth and so thankful to be in school [or to have this job.] I am working toward an amazing future."*

You can curse your day by thinking and speaking ill of it or you can choose to view your day's efforts as a privilege and an immense opportunity to act in furtherance of the only two things that really matter: learning and loving. If at the end of each day you accomplished some of both, it was a good day, no matter what.

Be hopeful when you speak about your day.

It actually takes more courage to be an optimist than it does to be a pessimist. To seek out cause for hopefulness is to risk disappointment. Be brave enough to be hopeful. Persist in that hopefulness no matter the temporary setbacks.

If the day was just not your day, remember that it is *the day that was.*

The great news is that tomorrow you get another chance to be better, stronger, wiser and kinder. Refuse to dwell on whatever went wrong earlier in the day, and where appropriate set about the task of self-correction. Maybe you were called on in class and you simply were not as well-prepared as you could have been. Resolve that the next time that you are in that class, you will get back in the game by being particularly well-prepared and raising your hand often so that your teacher sees your effort.

Maybe you said some unkind things to someone. Send that person an apology. Decide how you will make the situation better.

Maybe this simply was not meant to be your day. Like the baby's bib says, *"Spit happens."* If matters are within your control, fix them. Otherwise, look for the silver lining. It is there, even though that may not yet be readily apparent. Trust that you are protected, that the angels are cheering you on and that you are precisely where you are meant to be. Shift your focus away from all that is wrong to everything that is right. Sit quietly and make a gratitude list. A grateful heart will not have room for self-rebuke or second-guessing.

CHAPTER 33

How to Talk About Law School, Your Job and Your Life

Declare that you love the law, law school, your work and your life.

Your experiences in law school, at work, in love and in life will match your level of rhetoric about your experiences in law school, at work, in love and in life. The world rises (or falls) to meet your level of expectation. Every day, state emphatically that you love the law, law school, your job and the people in your life. Fake it until you make it. Sure enough and soon enough, reasons to be right about your declarations will start showing up.

Your experiences with anything or anyone will follow your thoughts and words. That is an important but subtle point to take to heart. What we think about and talk about most expands. What we think about and talk about most charts our path. I have devoted three decades to seeking out the virtue and great promise of our craft, our world and the people in it. Consistently, I have found that virtue. Even in the face of setbacks, I have persisted in believing and proclaiming that the law is a noble profession. My experiences have met me at that level of expectation. I have found honor and valor in the pursuit of justice.

An enthusiastic person will always have experiences to be excited about.

A loving person will live in a loving world. By contrast, an angry person will always have something to be angry about. The cynic will be vindicated in his cynicism. Choose to be the eternal optimist. To the extent that you are called a Pollyanna because of your hopefulness, say thank you. Pollyanna is one of the most mischaracterized figures. She was not the naïve, doe-eyed "yes" person that some try to portray. She was actually an exceedingly intelligent mediator and peacemaker. Her virtue and tenacity moved mountains. So will yours.

Do not confuse cynicism with discernment.

Do not make the mistake of confusing cynicism with discernment. Some will suggest that the world and the people in it are more often rotten than good. Do not believe that. It is simply not true.

The cynic's indictment is more than misguided. It is a form of cowardice. Be brave enough to believe that life is beautiful and that people are good. Know that even in the face of disappointment, you are strong enough not just to love, *but to persist in love.*

Be what you want to see.

Focus most on what you want more of. Do not dwell on what you want less of. When you are asked, *"How is law school?"* your response should be *"I love it!" "How are your classmates?" "I'm part of a community of good, high-minded people. They will be my colleagues and friends for life." "How are your classes?" "They are making me wiser and stronger every day."*

No matter where your studies or career path find you, do your work with passion. Declare your esteem for your classmates and co-workers. Proclaim your gratitude for the opportunities that this context is bringing into your life. No matter how seemingly humble your starting position happens to be, do all tasks with grace, dignity and elegance.

Persistently speaking good things about your life will bring more good things to speak about your life.

Extricate yourself from conversations that are not worthy of you. Fight the impulse to want to criticize the people in your midst or to speak badly about yourself. When something goes wrong, decline the temptation to want to talk about it again and again.

The choice to stay positive will require a steady resolve on your part. Our brains have been conditioned to go to worry and pessimism as the default settings. Retrain your mind by persistently thinking about and talking about what is going right.

You are the conductor and not a passenger on your train of thoughts.

Take the wheel and steer your thoughts in the direction of your dreams. Your thoughts are the predicates to your words, and your words ordain your actions. Choose what you think and what you say wisely. Your experiences will mirror back to you your level of rhetoric about them.

Do not wait for good things to happen before you talk about good things happening. Start now, wherever you are and whatever you are doing, to proclaim loudly and relentlessly all that you are happy about, excited about and thankful for. Be expansive and be generous in your estimations of yourself and others.

Instead of, *"I am so tired,"* try, *"I am so excited about this weekend, because I will get to catch up on some sleep."* Instead of, *"I am so fat,"* try, *"I am so excited about the new gym that just opened up near my apartment. Even if it's only for ten minutes at a time, I am getting on that treadmill because I am an athlete in training. It doesn't matter how fast I go. What matters is that I go,"* and instead of, *"I hate my job,"* try *"I am grateful to have this job, and every day as I seek out the good in this position I find it."*

It takes only three weeks to make a habit or break a habit. You can habituate positive thoughts by practicing them reliably for twenty-one days. You can create healthy habits by committing to them, persistently, for three weeks. That is a blink of an eye in the scheme of things. Decide now to be the boss of you and the manager of your life.

CHAPTER 34

How to Talk About Others

Do not talk about others unless you have something nice to say.

When you do have something nice to say be sure to say it. Be brave enough to make it a habit to communicate to people the admiration, esteem and respect that you have for them. It takes courage to do that because we are afraid that when we tell people the positive things that we think and feel about them they will think that we are a fake. Let go of that fear and know that if you are honest and authentic in your praise, you will be perceived as honest and authentic.

Compliment your classmates when they do good work in class. When a teacher inspires you, say so. When a colleague or adversary does an impressive job, learn from it and thank them for the opportunity to learn from it. When you observe an act of kindness, acknowledge it and talk about it. In school, at work and in life, if you admire qualities in another, communicate your appreciation. Do not let the naysayers dominate the discourse.

Contribute positively, allowing what you say to lift people up rather than bring them down.

Assume that everything that you say about another person is going to be repeated to that person and attributed to you.

Do not gossip. Too many bridges can be burned that way and too much drama generated. You do not have time for that nonsense. Do not say anything about another that you would not want repeated. If you find yourself about to say something that is petty or mean-spirited, stop yourself, even if it is in mid-sentence, and turn the statement into something positive. When you have something nice to say about another person, say it often. That too will be repeated and attributed to you. That is how bridges are built. It is also a way to assure that your life will run smoothly.

Do not talk *about* a person who has hurt your feelings. Talk *to* that person.

If someone has done something to upset you, wait until you are calm to choose whether and how to respond. Do not do or say anything while you are still angry. Your anger will make you stupid. Instead, cool off, not by venting but by going for a walk, a run or to the gym.

When you are back in your right mind, ask yourself whether the person who offended you is apt to be a recurrent part of your life. If the answer is yes, then get in touch with him or her. Reach out and speak your peace calmly and quietly. Give whomever it is the benefit of the doubt. Maybe she did not know better. Maybe it is all a big misunderstanding. Maybe he wanted to hurt you. Whatever the motivation, every intention has to return to its source. No doubt you have heard before that *what goes around comes around, we reap as we sow and every dog has his day.*

Those are truisms because they are true. A person who deliberately hurts others cannot help but hurt himself. What we do to others, we do to ourselves. You do not have to do anything to assure that result, in the same way that you do not have to do anything to make gravity work.

Remember that you cannot control anyone else's actions. You are the boss only of you. Take charge of your reactions. Explain your position, and then move on. Be informed by what the other person did or did not do, but do not be diminished by it. While it may have hurt you, it can only continue to hurt you if you let it. For your sake, let it go.

If someone has slighted you, do not complain to others about it.

Do not go to people other than the source of your displeasure to gossip or complain. *"But it's not gossiping,"* you protest. *"I am simply venting."* Ask yourself if that is really true. What is your real intention when you tell the story, whatever that story happens to be? Most likely, it is to put the offender in a bad light, to hurt him by compromising others' estimations of him while adding fuel to the fires of your indignation.

Again, remember that every intention returns to its source. When you act with the intent to hurt another, you cannot help but hurt yourself. For that matter, you have no control over what the people you have "vented" to will do with the information that you have shared. The material that you shared could be used to your great disadvantage. Your confidante might be anything but, and proceed to tell even more people about your tale of woe. As the story gets disseminated, it cannot help but get distorted at your expense. Moreover, it is no longer yours to remediate. If and when you and the offender make amends, the world at large is still involved and the matter lives on.

You do not want to compound any trespass against you by making it public knowledge. The matter is between you and the person who caused you offense. Take it up there, using the first person when you explain why you are hurt. For example, *"I learned that you said some unkind things about me and that hurt my feelings. I don't understand why you would do that. What happened?"* or *"I felt left out when I heard that you organized a night out but didn't invite me"* or *"I am disappointed that you never responded to my texts asking for the class notes that I missed."*

It takes courage to communicate your feelings, especially hurt feelings, to another. You have to be willing to be vulnerable. Take the chance and let the person know what is in your heart. You will grow stronger in character and spirit every time you stick up for yourself. By communicating that you have feelings and those feelings were hurt, you give others permission to follow your example to champion themselves. You give the person who hurt you a chance to explain, apologize and maybe even learn from the experience.

Most essentially, never respond to incivility in kind. Be a class act. Say what needs to be said, and go on your way. You have more important work to do than to dwell on another's misdeed or participate in another's low-mindedness.

PART 5

Finding Your Career Path, Applying for Jobs and Handling Rejection or Criticism

CHAPTER 35

You Do Not Need to Know What You Want to Do

Uncertainty is your greatest ally. Use it to stay receptive to all opportunities.

Maybe you know your desired career path. But it is more likely that you don't. Whether you have an idea of what you would like to do or not, remain open to all of the possibilities that a law degree provides. Say yes to every opportunity to use what you are learning to be of service to others. I assiduously cultivated that habit in law school and in the practice, and applied for every internship, externship, *pro bono* project, clinic, research assistantship, moot court, journal, student leadership post and teaching fellowship available. I served in the public sector and in the private sector. Each experience helped to inform what I would do next, and provided the basis for a process of elimination. I loved doing housing reform work, but was not well-suited to criminal prosecution or defense. I loved to teach, but did not have an aptitude for corporate transactional work. I was inspired by first amendment values and media defense work, but less so by securities fraud law.

It does not matter that you are unsure about what you would like to do with your degree. In fact, that uncertainty is your biggest ally. Use it to stay receptive to all opportunities. Say yes to every chance to serve. For every endeavor, try to be the most prepared person in the room.

Commit wholeheartedly to the task that is right in front of you. Be guided by the people you admire. Ask to be used for a purpose mightier than yourself. Do all that, and your calling will find you.

Diversify your portfolio.

In school take lots of different classes and at work try lots of different contexts in which to serve. I began law school with the vague inkling that I would be doing public interest criminal defense work. I spent a semester doing just that for a criminal justice clinic and quickly realized that the context was not well-suited to my strengths. I worked on behalf of Volunteer Lawyers for the Arts and I loved that work, because it involved lots of negotiating and contract drafting. When I served low-income tenants and displaced families on behalf of Morningside Heights Legal Services, I knew that housing reform would become a part of my life's work.

Think of law school as presenting you with a vast buffet of classes and experiences to choose from. Do not be a picky eater. Fill your plate with gusto and with an open mind. Try new things. By a process of elimination, you will come to know what you love, what you like and what is simply not for you. Once in the practice, join your local and state bar associations and get involved. Join a team on a worthy *pro bono* initiative. Volunteer to serve on committees. That way, you make connections and build your stores of social capital.

Seek out mentors.

Attend panel presentations, guest lectures, symposia and lots of receptions and events where you are likely to be in the presence of people whom you aspire to be like. Seek them out as mentors. Be forthright and introduce yourself, or ask one of your professors or colleagues to help you to make the introduction. Ask people you admire to be your mentors. Meet with them, seek to shadow them at work for a day, learn how they got to do what they do and let their example inform your own path.

Go to bar association events. Students sometimes can attend at no cost or, at least, at a reduced cost. Volunteer to work at the events, at the reception table. That way, you get to attend at no cost and you quite naturally get to meet and greet everyone who arrives, giving you a way to resume conversation later in the evening.

Stay on purpose.

Stay on purpose by seeking out ways to serve. Show up by giving 100% to everything that you do. Stay alert and be present. Your calling—the work that makes your heart sing—will speak to you, sometimes loudly but often in the form of a whisper. Be attentive enough to hear its call. Believe that you were born for a purpose even mightier than you could have imagined, and know that your path will rise up to lead you to it.

You Deserve to Be Happy

When you find what you love, do it.

Joseph Campbell famously said, *"Follow your bliss."* Do what you love. There is nothing selfish or hedonistic about making yourself happy. Your happiness serves the world. Every atrocity committed in the course of human history has been committed by people who were miserable. Cultivate joy, and fill your life with so much exuberance that the spillover cannot help but improve the lives of others.

Be the star of your own life, and not a supporting actor in someone else's life story.

I remember hearing one of the members of the famous Rat Pack (the group of celebrities who traveled with Frank Sinatra) observe, *"It's Frank's world. We just get to live in it."* Make your life *yours*. Do not be a hanger-on or simply a member of someone else's entourage. Follow your dreams, not someone else's.

Be big in the world.

Be big not in the way that Hollywood might define the term, but big in terms of your benevolence, generosity of spirit and magnanimity. Be the most interested person in every room. Be loud in your praise of others. Be reliably kind. Seek out every opportunity to share your success.

Do all that and watch what happens. You will grow in stature, influence, opportunity and goodwill. Others will see you as the aspiration statement and find hope in your example. Your success will be assured and, even more, your significance will set the world aflame.

CHAPTER 37

The Interview: How to Be When You Want to Make a Good First Impression

Cultivate a posture of optimism.

Political strategists coach candidates to think two thoughts before making a public appearance: 1) *I am really happy to be here* and 2) *I have a secret*. The former is based on the premise that people are drawn to and trust those who are optimistic. The latter endeavors to cultivate on the actor's part an expression of brimming expectancy. That expression generates in the viewer's mind's eye the impression that this person is interesting and has something to tell me and perhaps even to teach me.

Try that technique just before you go in for a job interview, a networking reception, a presentation and any other setting in which you aim to make a good first impression. In the mirror, practice thinking, "*I am so happy to be here*" and "*I have a secret.*" Notice how your smile becomes slightly impish and how your eyes start to twinkle. Behavioral psychologists confirm that the viewer's more primitive brain receptors (the medulla and cerebellum) will translate that body language into, *"Oh, I want to know what this person knows."*

Be the most interested person in the room.

If you are going for a job interview, know in advance as much as you can about your potential employer. Learn about the firm or company and learn about the person who will be interviewing you. Prepare in advance three questions that you would like to ask the interviewer.

When I was in private practice, I served as a recruiter for the law firm. Always, at the end of each interview, I would ask, *"Do you have any questions?"* If the interview was thorough, sometimes the answer was no. But more often than not, it mattered to me that the interviewee had taken the time and care to prepare some questions. It mattered that the person before me was interested in learning more and had done the research to have a basis for meaningful exchange.

Think in advance of three characteristics about yourself that you would like to communicate.

For example, you want to make clear that you are exceedingly hard-working, a great researcher and a very strong writer. Other traits to emphasize include: you are a team player, you enjoy working with people, you were raised with a very strong work ethic, you are loyal and you understand the importance of discretion. You are a person of integrity, and you endeavor to do all things with character and strength of purpose. You follow-up on all tasks and you bring a deep love of learning to every project.

On the day of the given interview or networking event, make sure that you have read the news and are up on current events.

Your knowledge of current events can fill in any otherwise awkward lulls in the conversation and can help you to respond meaningfully if the interviewer happens to bring up some recent newsworthy event. I read the New York Times every morning (like it or not, it is the paper of record for the world. Read it.) I remember going in for an interview on a Tuesday (that's the day that the Times contains the Science section.) Thankfully, I had read that day's Science section, and could venture a response when the interviewer began the interview by asking a question that was based on that section's story about the melting Arctic ice cap.

If discussing current events, avoid hot topics like politics and religion. Do not ascribe labels to yourself, such as *"I'm a Republican, or Democrat, or Libertarian, or liberal or conservative"* and the list goes on. Kierkegaard was right that *"If you label me, you negate me."* You want to avoid giving others the opportunity to tune you out or make snap judgments about you based on some label.

If you are attending a networking reception or other business or social occasion where it will be more difficult to prepare, simply show up and be interested.

Be brave enough to introduce yourself to people, and as you meet them, be interested in learning their story. Who are they? What do they do? Let the conversation flow organically and use your emotional intelligence to determine how best to jump into that flow. Has the discussion turned to the topic of great meals?

Then talk about a new restaurant that you are hoping to try. Did someone mention the HBO series *Homeland?* If you watch it, join in. If you do not, ask questions about it.

During a lull in the conversation, introduce some interesting or recently trending event. Think in advance of topics that might make for light-hearted conversational fare. (Again, avoid lightning-rod, controversial issues.) For example, if you just saw a wonderful movie, talk about that (unless it happens to be one of the installments in the *Jackass* series.) You might ask whether anyone in the group happened to see that story about how Chinese zookeepers are dressing up like pandas to help the animals acclimate to the wilderness. (People love pandas. Read up on them so that when someone in the group exclaims, *"I love pandas,"* you can respond with your panda trivia. Believe it or not, that is the sort of banter that will make you memorable when you follow up with the people you met.)

Take nothing personally.

If the interviewer or potential contact that you approach seems dismissive or curt, do not take it personally. It could be that she is preoccupied by an email that she just received, or is running behind schedule or simply not feeling well. Do not let your insecurities run amok to try to convince you that you screwed up, she did not like you, you are inadequate and a flop and so on. Say, *"I tried my best,"* and move on.

Sometimes what you think was your worst interview was actually your best.

When I was in law school, I interviewed for a judicial clerkship with a jurist I admired immensely. I prepared exceedingly well, had several points that I hoped to communicate about myself and several questions that I wanted to present to the justice. At the interview, the justice spoke for fifteen minutes about his approach to the jurisprudential challenges of the more difficult cases. It was a brilliant exposition, and all I could think of to do was to nod studiously. At the end of his narrative, he stood and said, *"It was a pleasure meeting you. You will be hearing from me soon."* It was clear that the interview was over, and that there was no opportunity for me to interject with questions or talking points. I shook the justice's hand and left his chambers feeling dejected.

On the entire ride back home, I engaged in multiple variations of self-criticism. *"Why didn't you interject meaningfully?"* I asked myself. I did not interject because there really did not seem to be an opportunity to do that, but my emotion-based tirade could not acknowledge that reality. *"Why did you just sit there like a deer in headlights?"* Actually, I was attentive throughout. *"Why didn't you ask the questions you had prepared?"* I did not prolong the interview because the justice seemed to be in a rush to move on to something else.

When I returned home, I received a call from the justice. He said, *"It was a pleasure to meet you today. I'm sorry that we couldn't speak longer, but there was an emergent matter that I had to get to. I am calling because I would like to offer you the job."* It turned out that my instincts were right after all. During the interview, there was neither the time nor the opportunity for me to say or do more. Over time, I learned to trust those instincts, rather than resort to second-guessing or harsh self-judgments.

With patience and experience, you will learn that sometimes less is more. To get to the next opportunity, you do not always have to say everything that you had planned to say or do everything that you had planned to do. Sometimes you do not have to do or say anything to be placed precisely where you are meant to be.

I believe that each of us has a path and a destiny. Ask to be used for a purpose that is mighty and honorable. Seek to use your gifts to bring joy to the world. Be of service. Use your words and actions to ease the suffering of others. Continue to show up as a compassionate force for the good. Ask to be found precisely where you need to be and your calling will find you. Expect great things. Life will meet you at that level of expectation.

CHAPTER 38

What to Remember When You Are Rejected or Criticized

When you are rejected, it is because you are protected.

Rejection means that the given position, placement or person was not meant for you. Trust that to be true, because it is the truth. With the benefit of time's passage, you will come to know that for sure. For now, take it as a matter of faith. What is meant to be for you will be for you. You will run into trouble when you chase a path or a person that does not belong to you.

Do not pursue someone else's dream. Do not compare yourself with others. That will only yield resentment or arrogance. What comes to others is their business, not yours. Be happy for others' success. Know that success is infinite. It is limitless, and the best way to assure your own is to be happy for others' victories.

As you celebrate others' achievements and decide to be governed by what you want (rather than by what you do not want), you set in motion a set of thoughts and then actions to help you to realize those desires. Your life will always move in the direction of your dominant thoughts and actions.

To be governed by your resentments or jealousies will assure a basis for even more bitterness. To be guided by the wins—yours and others'—assures more wins. That is what the truism *"nothing succeeds like success"* means. It is a truism because it is true.

Take rejection in stride.

If no one is rejecting you, you are playing it too safe. That is true in life and in love. Cast out a line, even if it feels like a long-shot, and see what comes back. You miss every chance that you do not take. Take the shot. Do your best, and if you miss, learn from the experience. Be self-corrective. Maybe you need to modify your approach. Make the necessary modifications and get back in the game.

Any form of critique or criticism is simply information.

Criticism is information. It can help you to make adjustments and modifications that render your work and performance stronger. Several years ago one of my finest research assistants was in his second year of law school and assisting me with a law review article. I marked up his research memo and then completely re-worked it to arrive at the central thesis for the piece. To his great credit, he took none of that personally and saw it instead for what it was: helpful and constructive feedback. He internalized the editing and learned from it. Later, he said, *"The give and take on this project has made me such a better writer. Thank you for that."* By checking his ego at the door, he made the process of working with him a pleasure. Moreover, he spared himself (and me) the drama that our insecurities can sometimes create. His positive attitude, relentless work ethic and fine abilities have assured his success as he has since advanced from one esteemed position in the law to the next.

Do not let praise or rebuke go to your head.

Be thankful for all forms of feedback, but do not let any of it go to your head. Do not allow negative feedback to devastate you, and do not let positive feedback inflate your ego. Cultivate the discernment to know which critiques are worthy of self-reflection and which are best left with their giver.

Neutralize the critic's power to potentially throw you off your game by taking a step back and asking first, is this criticism offering relevant information about you or, instead, about the critic? Often, our judgments about others are actually judgments about ourselves. You may have heard the expression that when we point a finger, three fingers are pointing back at us. What that means is that we tend to project our own perceived deficiencies or inadequacies onto others. With time, you will develop the capability to know when to accept another's judgment and when to reject it.

The tale of the sage: Know which criticisms actually belong to their giver.

There is the parable of the sage, an elder in her community who was well known for her capacity to respond to struggle and conflict with grace. A more cynical member of the community attempted repeatedly to diminish the wise woman's achievements and to mock her message. Throughout, the woman declined to respond or to defend herself, until one day the critic came to her front door to once again launch into his litany of criticisms. Finally, the sage answered. She said, *"Sir, if someone offers you a gift, but you decline to accept it, the gift belongs to whom?"* The hostile young man paused, and then replied, *"It belongs to the person who offered it." "Precisely,"* said the elder. She continued, *"Similarly, if I decline to accept your criticisms and harsh judgments, to whom do they then belong?"* The man was left speechless, never to return again.

Cultivate discernment.

Discernment is the ability to know which criticisms to accept and which to leave with their giver. It is the wisdom to know when your self-talk is actually parroting someone else's voice that you internalized long ago but that never belonged to you. For example, when you criticize yourself for something, who do you sound like? Gently return that voice to its speaker. Find your own voice, and use it to champion yourself and the people, causes and virtues that you stand for.

It is important that you take good care in determining which of the criticisms to come your way belong more to their giver than to you. Similarly, exercise care in your judgments of others. *You cannot admire or detest something about another person unless it reflects something that you love or hate about yourself.*

CHAPTER 39

Know Your Worth

Remember that you are not what you are called. You are what you answer to.

Inequities persist. All -*isms*, or systems of advantage based on some fixed characteristic, plaque the legal profession just as they do society at large. Whether manifested in the form of racism (a system of advantage based on race), sexism (a system of advantage based on gender), classism (a system of advantage based on socioeconomic status), or any other form of bias, barriers to equal access persist. Particularly when in the presence of any attempt to invalidate your experiences, demean your worth or make you feel invisible, teach people how to treat you. Be clear about what you will and will not answer to.

The challenges that face women

There is still a glass ceiling and there continue to be forces aimed at denigrating women's power and devaluing women's worth. See what needs to be seen and respond with a clarity of vision, compassion and cohesiveness that declares firmly, "*Call me assertive, but I won't answer to bitch. Call me a game-changer, but I won't answer to obstinate. Call me kind and generous, but I won't answer to people-pleaser. Call me busy and multidimensional, but I won't answer to 'not fully on board'. Call me an essay in grace under pressure, but I won't answer to frazzled."*

To repudiate feminism is to misunderstand it. It is the pursuit of equal opportunity, a pursuit that is all the more urgent in the midst of a rollback of previous gains to achieve parity of income and access. That access is still denied in countless venues and attempts persist, some more insidious than others, to invalidate and demean women and girls.

That devaluation is present every time the message is communicated, *"You can go this high, but no higher."* It is present in the pejoratives that are ascribed to any form of perceived weakness. *"Don't be such girls,"* the coach tells the young men on his team. It is there on the less than level playing field of interpersonal relationships that describes a man as a *"player"* and a woman as a *"skank."* All of those rebukes and characterizations distort what it means to be female and poison girls' and boys' perceptions of gender-based differences.

Do not say unkind things about yourself (or anyone else).

In all areas of your life, avoid holding yourself or another to some standard of perfection. The beauty industry invests countless billions of dollars every year on advertising campaigns whose aim is to make people feel inadequate. Models are air-brushed and photo-shopped to represent a standard of beauty that is physically impossible and a conceptualization of thinness that is unhealthy. When we look at the images and realize that we are not that, we buy their products with the hope that maybe we will get closer to the aesthetic that they are peddling.

Studies show that the greater the degree of a girl or woman's internalization of the industry standard of beauty the lesser the degree of her political efficacy. Think about how many times you have held yourself back because you thought it was a bad hair day, or you felt fat. Think about what you say to yourself when you look in the mirror. How many times have you said of yourself or to yourself, *"I am a hot mess,"* or *"I am so bloated,"* or *"I look so terrible."* Catch yourself in that moment and say instead, *"If I am kind, generous and loving today, I am beautiful."* Snap out of your self-consciousness and decide to be present and fully seen for the goodness and talents that reside inside of you. No one else would hold you to as harsh a standard as you no doubt hold yourself. Be joyfully you, because that is what will capture people's hearts and minds.

Do not surrender your power to a bad hair day.

Listen carefully to your self-talk. How mean are you to yourself? Would you ever be that cruel to another? Think about how often you have sabotaged your day because you did not like the way you looked or maybe your pants felt tight or you got a huge pimple. Your male counterparts are most likely not trying to be invisible because of a break-out or frizz.

I remember telling my mom about a presentation that I had given, where I had talked about the promise of good government and ethics reform. As I described the talk I also told my mother, *"I don't think I looked good. My suit had gotten wrinkled on the train and my hair was awful."* My mom asked, *"Were you loving throughout the course of the event?"* I answered that I was. *"In that case,"* she said, ***"you were beautiful."***

CHAPTER 40

You Are Already Good

No external source can be the judge of your worth. Know that you are already good.

Whenever you confront or embrace any criticism, what you are really trying to know is whether or not you are good. You await feedback from a professor to know whether you are a good student. You receive evaluations from an employer to know whether you are a good worker. You await your child's words to know whether you are a good parent. Here is the problem with framing criticism or feedback as a way of discerning whether or not you are good: No external source, whether a teacher, employer, co-worker, friend, classmate, spouse, parent or child, can ever be the judge of your worth. To give anyone or anything the power to define you or chart your course puts you at the mercy of another's lens of perception. That lens cannot help but be distorted by the biases of the beholder.

It is up to you to know, *really know*, that you are already good. You were born that way, and you will stay that way. You are better, so much better, than the worst thing you have ever done.

You have shined brightly and you have fallen flat. Your finest moment is yet to be. Through it all, you have been good.

Do not subject your estimation of the measure of your significance to the carelessness of the crowds.

People can be reckless and irresponsible sometimes. Do not hang yourself out in the marketplace of public opinion to arrive at your sense of self-worth. If you look to external feedback to gauge your intrinsic value, you will be flapping in the changing winds of others' impressions. You are magnificent because you are. Get that through your head and your heart because if you don't, you will be chasing others' approval when you should be chasing your dreams.

You will come to see your intrinsic worth by keeping in touch with your soul. Seek out daily sanctuaries, whether found in nature, in a chapel or any other quiet place, or by reading inspiring words, meditating, listening to moving music, practicing yoga, going for a walk or volunteering at a local children's hospital. To remember your innate goodness, spend some time sitting with newborn babies. Be in awe of the divinity in every face, whether of a child, an elder and everyone in between. The beauty that you perceive in others is the same beauty inside of you.

Return to your own answer to the question *who do you think you are?*

In the presence of any feedback, whether good or bad, always return to your answer to the question *who do you think you are?* Keep the answer to that question close at hand, whether on an index card or on your phone. Let it resound with the truth about you.

You are a person of substance and honor. You are a champion of the underdog and a voice for those you have yet to find their own. You are a giver of hope because your life bears living witness to the essential premise that what does not kill us makes us stronger. You understand criticism for what it is: feedback that has the potential to improve your performance at something. Sometimes that feedback is helpful. Other times it is best left with its giver. Regardless, no evaluation can ever be taken as a referendum on the measure of your worth. The inviolate truth about you persists and is unassailable: You are worthy, you are significant and you are good. Not because of what you did or did not do, but because you are.

PART 6

How to Handle Conflict or Adversity

CHAPTER 41

What You Need to Remember in the Face of a Slight or Betrayal

Another's meanness is their business, not yours.

There is an inviolate, untouchable part of you that no one can ever diminish. When someone tries to hurt you, be like a puppy that gets caught in the rain. Shake it off and keep going. Refuse to hold onto the snub or insult and leave it with its giver. That is where it belongs and that is where it cannot help but end up.

The person who meant to hurt you will suffer as a consequence of his or her hurtful actions. You do not have to do anything to assure that result, just as you do not have to do anything to assure that the apple you drop will fall to the ground. Like the law of gravity, the law of cause and effect is always at work. Every action runs as a cause and must return to its originator as an effect.

Whatever we do to others we do to ourselves.

Whatever we do to others, we do to ourselves, in the same way that whatever we do *for* others we do for ourselves. Call it karma, the boomerang effect or the law of just desserts, but the point remains: Every intention returns to its source. The expressions *"every dog has his day," "what goes around comes around"* and *"we reap as we sow"* are truisms because they are true. When you intend to hurt another, you will inescapably bring hurt to yourself.

We do not get what we want. We get what we are.

In a world of infinite possibilities, remember that we do not get what we want. *We get what we are.* A hurtful person will live in a hurtful world. A loving person will live in a loving world. Give what you want to receive.

For that very reason, decline the temptation to respond to meanness or incivility in kind. The antidote to another's mean-spiritedness is never more of the same. The corrective for heartlessness is love. Love yourself enough that you refuse to carry around another's wrongdoing by holding on to a grudge or a grievance, or reliving the episode a thousand times in your mind's eye.

For your sake, and for the sake of the countless people, clients and constituencies who are counting on you to make the difference that only you can make as a person of principle and virtue, *let it go.* Drop the chip on your shoulder. It will only weigh you down.

CHAPTER 42

Be an Instrument of Peace

Take the high road.

Sometimes, you will find yourself at odds with a teacher, classmate, employer, colleague, adversary, family member, neighbor or friend. Know this, first and foremost: Your intention is the most powerful tool that you bring to any dispute or discord. Set your intention before you say another word to that person or about that person.

Do your words and actions intend to stir the pot of trouble or sow the seeds of understanding? Is what you are about to say intended to cause hurt to that person or to promote forgiveness? Remember that an intention has to return to its source. Whatever you intend, ultimately, is what you get in return. If you intend to cause pain, you will receive pain. If you intend to bring peace, you will receive peace. Thus, be clear and be high-minded about your intent.

Set as your intention the desire to promote the cause of mutual understanding, respect and goodwill. It takes only one person to defuse a conflict and to turn anger into reason and fear into calm. By contrast, to respond to meanness with more meanness is, simply put, beneath you. You are too good for that.

"But," you might protest, "I am right about this, and he is wrong. What he did was wrong, what he said was wrong, and what he failed to say was wrong." Maybe you are right about everything. But as the old saying goes, you can be right or you can be happy. Choose to be happy. Trust me on that. Let it go, take the high road and hold onto your perception of the agitator as he could be once he heeds the call of his better instincts. Do that and you help him to answer to that call. Meet him instead at his level of lesser virtue and you only make matters worse.

Do not take the bait.

The fish is caught because of its mouth. When someone dangles a worm of offense, refuse to bite. Take very good care with your words. Otherwise, you will only say or do something best left unsaid and undone. Keep swimming.

Never fight with a skunk.

I recently gave a talk where I cautioned against responding to meanness in kind. Afterward, Gerald Viturello, a public servant, shared the wisdom of his former colleague to "never fight with a skunk." That says it all. If you take on the skunks, you take on the stink. Walk away.

Getting stuck in resentment robs you of your power.

Hanging on to negative judgments deprives you of the opportunity to see what is really good in your midst. Holding on to resentment puts you at the mercy of another's incivility. Do not demean yourself by responding to meanness in kind. Try to be the voice of reason and, if that fails, walk away rather than do something you will regret. Never send an email in anger, and never reduce to writing what you would not want broadcast on the nightly news.

CHAPTER 43

Let Your Kindness Be Irresistible

Show up with a basket of muffins.

Before entering any situation that is fraught, anchor yourself in so much dignity, grace and goodness that, just by showing up, you elevate the room. Be generous and be kind. Show up with a basket of muffins or a bouquet of flowers. Your humanity will be disarming, and your presence will encourage others to show their kinder selves.

See the agitator as better than whatever he or she is doing right now.

Stubbornly persist in your capacity to see the given agitator as better than whatever he is displaying at the moment. When a colleague or adversary does something unbecoming, calmly say to him, *"I know that you are a gentleman and a good lawyer."* Then walk away. Allow for some breathing space and let some time pass. Soon you will see that your decision to be generous in that moment was not only disarming but transformative.

Do not hold onto any indignity by thinking about it or talking about it.

Do not hold onto any agitator's trespass by continuing to replay it in your mind or by repeating it to others. Let the person who behaved poorly off the hook. How he behaved is his business and his mess. How you respond is your business. Take the high road. Free yourself from the need to convince others of how awful he is. That kind of talk will only reflect poorly on you. His words and actions will speak for themselves, and he will reap the consequences of his conduct. You do not have to do anything to assure that result. Do not dwell on what he did or did not do. Move on. You have more important matters to think about and more important work to do.

CHAPTER 44

Power versus Force

How to be persuasive

True persuasion comes from the effective use of your power rather than force. Power comes from within. It is the quiet knowing that rightness is on your side and that it will prevail. Anchored in careful preparation and restraint, it is exercised gently and to great effect.

Force, by contrast, is rooted in insecurity. It is externally-derived and can quickly devolve into coercion or, worse, brutality. It is combustible and as it explodes it becomes scattered and diffused, thereby losing precision. While it might temporarily secure certain aims, its ends are short-lived because they lack the power of legitimacy.

Use your power to calmly bring others to your point of view, no matter how long that might take. State your peace forthrightly and without hesitation. Allow for the other to rant and rave if he is so inclined. Wait for the tantrum to be done. As it spills out all over the place, do not defend and do not push back. Remember that you are using power, not force. Extricate yourself from the scene until the storm has passed and then, with the same equipoise and calm, re-state your position and your desired end.

The first person to raise his voice has lost the argument.

Our anger makes us stupid. You lose all power to persuade when you move from your rational mind into your emotion mind. Believe in the rightness of your cause and then, like a surgeon at work, be precise and deliberate in your execution. Do not allow your ego to cloud your judgment, and do not be deceived into thinking that you must fight *against* something or someone. *Remember what you are fighting for and be for that, not against something else.*

An esteemed jurist recently used the metaphor of buying a car to tell our students about the virtues of the quiet exercise of power. Suppose that you have done the research and that you have come up with the amount that you are willing to pay for a particular car make and model. Be sure that your number is reasonable and fair. Go into the dealership, and present your research and your number to the dealer. Suppose that your aim is to buy the car with certain enumerated features for $30,000. The dealer might launch into a detailed recitation of all the reasons why your number is too low, and then he might engage in verbal and mathematical acrobatics to convince you why you need to raise that number. Sit tight and do not refute or defend against anything that he is saying. When he is done, calmly state, *"I will buy the car with the features enumerated for $30,000."* Then just sit there quietly. More often than not, when all is said and done you will prevail on your terms.

CHAPTER 45

How to Break Bad News

The sandwich technique

Whenever you have to share bad news, use the sandwich technique. I learned this from one of my beloved teachers, Chara Caldarone. The first slice of bread is some bit of good or positive news that is relevant to the matter at hand. Next, state the bad news simply and without drama. That's the inside of the sandwich. Then, restate the good or positive news, making it the top slice of bread to complete the sandwich.

For example, suppose that you need to tell your parents about a lackluster grade. Start with the good news. *"Mom, Dad, I'm really enjoying law school and I did so well with moot court that one of the judges asked me to send him my resume for a summer job."* You have just set a positive backdrop against which the not so great grade is put into a larger perspective—your fine aptitude and promise in the law. Then state the bad news plainly. *"I got back my Torts grade, and ended up with a C. I'm disappointed but I made an appointment to see the professor and I'm looking forward to figuring out what happened and how I can do better."* Finish with more good news. *"Thank you for believing in me. I am committed to becoming a great lawyer and to working even harder than before to make you proud."*

The sandwich technique allows you to put your best foot forward and to conclude on that note. It works in both professional and personal realms. For example, suppose that you need to tell your client, a buyer of real estate, that the closing date on an investment piece of property has to be delayed by a week. Start with the good news. *"I am excited about closing this transaction for you. Having done the due diligence, this lot has been deemed a very solid investment."* Now break the bad news. *"I know that you are anxious to close, but I just heard from seller's counsel and we need to delay the closing by a week."* Then, conclude with the good news, *"By agreeing to the postponement, we have added leverage in the following ways."*

More personally, suppose that you have to break a dinner date. Start with the good news. *"Our friendship means so much to me. Thank you for always being there for me."* Then, *"I am so sorry but I am impossibly tied up on a deadline and I need to ask if we can please reschedule our dinner."* Close with, *"I can't wait to see you. As soon as you check your calendar, let's reschedule, sooner rather than later."*

CHAPTER 46

How to Cope With Competing Demands

You do not have to do it all and you certainly do not have to do it all at once.

If you find yourself answering to several competing demands, take a triage approach and respond to the most pressing matter first, and then continue to do what you can with the less immediate concerns. Know that you cannot be all things to all people and that you do not have to do everything that needs to be done all at the same time. For that matter, you cannot do it alone. Seek out help and support from those around you. Asking for help is not a sign of weakness. It is a show of strength. It indicates that you have the wisdom to know that no one can do it alone.

Find a good counselor or therapist to help you to cope with the difficult task of managing competing demands. It is important to have someone in your corner who can really listen to you and help to correct your perceptions when they become distorted by your own sheer exhaustion. Most schools have very helpful therapists who come to campus at least one day a week. They are licensed professionals who are obliged to keep all that you discuss confidential and privileged.

Stay away from energy suckers.

Sometimes people will try to sap your reserves of time and energy to replenish their own. Set healthy boundaries and extricate yourself from relationships that are draining. Think of the very word *draining*. You want to surround yourself with people running on a full tank, rather than those who try to siphon off yours.

Your competence in the world makes you a better family member, parent, child, friend and spouse.

Let your developing proficiencies make you even more generous in every role that you play. Allow your work ethic and growing confidence to inspire others. You are modeling all sorts of behaviors all of the time. See every context that you serve as a context for you to grace by your example.

CHAPTER 47

When You or a Family Member Gets Sick

Do not become an island.

Reach out to others. Tell your school's dean of students what is happening so that the two of you can anticipate what if any accommodations might need to be made to help you to get through the semester. Reach out to your classmates, co-workers and friends. Let them know what you are going through. They will rise to the challenge and carry you over the icy patches.

Do not keep your pain or sorrow to yourself. Everyone has experienced their share of heartache, and from that well of experience people will extend a hand. Accept others' help without hesitation or any form of embarrassment or shame. You will not be seen as *less than* because of your struggles. Indeed, you will be seen as *more than* whatever others thought before.

Give people a chance to be kind and generous to you, for their sake as much as for yours. Trust that a broken heart has more room, and that love brings hope.

CHAPTER 48

When You Endure the Break-Up of a Relationship

You will love again.

When the person you thought you were really crazy about decides to move on, ***know that anyone who does not want you does not deserve to have you.*** Who that person chooses to love or not love is his or her business. You cannot control that. You never did. We only let in the love we think we deserve. You cannot fix another.

When you have loved deeply, no matter the end, you are better because of it. Be gentle with your broken heart, and trust that you will love again. You will love again because you never stopped loving. To love is your essential nature. Do not wait for Mr. or Ms. Right to come walking through the door. Be the loving person that you are in all circumstances and in every context. That is how you get to be the star of your own life. It is charisma, and it will draw to you even more to love.

Do not become cynical about love.

Continue to believe in love. It will disappoint you sometimes, but be brave enough to know that you can transcend love's sorrows to once again bask in its glory. The measure of your greatness will not be found simply because you loved. The measure of your greatness will reside in your capacity *to persist* in loving, no matter the disenchantments and the setbacks.

You will get knocked down in the pursuit of love, but you will get back up. You will be called a starry-eyed idealist, and you will say *thank you*. The pessimist cannot answer to that call because he won't take the chance. Instead, he will stick to his story that life is a school of hard knocks and people stink. That way, he thinks, he cannot be hurt or disappointed. *But here is the tragedy of the cynic: By closing himself off to the power and promise of hopefulness, he suffers the greatest hurt of all—its loss. Keep hope alive in your heart. Without it, you join the ranks of the living dead.*

PART 7

How to Succeed on Exams and What to Do When You Feel Worried, Unsure or a Flop at the Task at Hand

CHAPTER 49

Exam Preparation and Peace of Mind

Ignore the craziness in the atmosphere.

Law school, and especially exam time, can do strange things to ordinarily kind, decent people. Competition can be fostered among some. Others retreat, feeling alienated. Some become aggressive, others cranky, and still others fatalistic. Extricate yourself from the doomsday prognosticators and ignore the hysteria and hype that the law exam mystique can conjure up. You have taken many, many tests before, and you have succeeded. The skills that served you well in the past will serve you well now.

Exams, and especially the first set of law school exams, can cause even the most capable people to doubt themselves. Recognize that to the extent that you are feeling uneasy, anxious or maybe even terrified, it is not you. The entire system of law school evaluation leaves much to be desired. It has built into it features destined to inspire panic. A whole semester's worth of work comes down to performance on a three or four hour exam. The law school exam itself—a series of hypotheticals—enjoys a

217

certain mystique, asking you to apply what you have learned to an unfamiliar context.

For that matter, there is an infectious contagiousness to pre-exam anxiety. You can catch it in the halls, the library and before and after class. You may walk into school on a Monday morning after a great weekend only to hear from a classmate, "*I just finished all of my outlines and synthesized Contracts. What a relief!*" Indeed. At that point, your uneasiness may be compounded by your wondering what an outline really is. An outline is simply a summary of the course, organized according to the units that the class covered. It is not rocket science, and it requires that you use organizational skills that you already possess.

Play your game, not someone else's.

You have prepared for exams before. Be true to the techniques that have served you well in the past. Do not compare your progress with others' progress. Take what others are saying about what they are doing and how they are doing it with a grain of salt. Play your game, not theirs.

You have the time you need.

Right about now you might be feeling that no matter how hard you work, there is just too much to do. Especially at those moments, remind yourself that these are conquerable matters. There are many hours in a day, and many minutes in an hour. You have the time you need.

Performance is enhanced by calm.

If and when you go into panic-mode, reassure yourself that you only need to survive. You do not need to get As. You need to pass. Set the bar modestly because the truth is, with each passing grade you are one step closer to becoming an attorney. Not an A, B, C or D lawyer, but a lawyer.

Panic comes when you hold yourself to some idealized standard of perfection. Get that impossible ideal out of your head because it doesn't exist. Keep moving through the material, knowing that your work only has to be as good as it can be under the totality of circumstances in which you find yourself. Under better circumstances, your work will be better. With time, as you become a stronger writer and test-taker, your work will improve. Do your best with the time that you have, knowing that this is simply your best *at this time*. With experience, you will continue to get better and better.

Be generous to your classmates.

Anxiety and nervousness is natural. But you can rise above it. For that matter, you can let it bring out the very best in you. It was Hemingway who defined guts as grace under pressure. Be generous to the people in your midst. Help them. Let a spirit of cooperation characterize all of your efforts, especially now. Reject any limited view of success. Success is infinite and it is contagious. There is plenty to go around.

Be kind, compassionate, and dignified, mindful that your classmates today will be your colleagues tomorrow. This legal community of ours is a small one, and people's memories are long. Know that one year from now, indeed, twenty years from now, your classmates won't remember you as the person who got two As or two Cs first semester. What they will remember is how you conducted yourself in the process. It is who you are, and how you got there, that they will remember.

For guidance on how to conduct yourself, think about what you would want said about you at your funeral. (No, exams won't kill you. But this exercise is actually a helpful one.) Our lives are not shaped by what we take with us, but by what we leave behind. When all is said and done, how would you want to be remembered? More immediately, at the conclusion of your law school years, what will you have left behind? What will be your legacy? Will they be saying, *"What a competitive, win at all costs kind of guy he was. I'll never forget the time he hid that outline from his study group."* Or will you be remembered as a decent, honest, hard-working person, always willing to help when you could? Memories die hard. The professional associations that you are forging now will outlive the challenges of the next few months.

CHAPTER 50

How to Be When You Feel Worried, Unsure, or Inadequate

Remember that feelings are not facts.

Say that out loud and believe it. Emotions are ephemeral. They come and go as long as you allow them to. When a feeling of dread or worry comes up, recognize that you are in emotion mind. Go back to rational mind by becoming analytical about the feeling, testing its legitimacy. For example, when emotion mind takes over and you find yourself thinking or speaking in absolutes such as *"I can't do this. There's too much here and I'll never get it done,"* gently challenge the thought by analytically testing it. Think, *"Wait a minute. You have gotten even more than this done in the past, and you have succeeded. This is conquerable. You don't have to move this mountain with one push. Let's start by removing one rock at a time."* That deductive process takes you out of emotion mind and back into your right mind.

You will know that you are in emotion mind when you are thinking and speaking in dramatic generalizations. For instance, *"I have no idea what's going on in class."* Realize that your hyper-generalization is untrue. You do have some idea of what is going on in class. If it is a Torts class that finds you confused, and more specifically, it is the material on proximate cause that is giving you trouble, you do know the context that you need help with. That knowledge gives you enough of a basis to reach out to the professor and to upper class students for tutoring, supplemental reading and whatever other assistance might prove helpful.

Do not *"should"* on yourself.

Sometime you will hear yourself saying, *"I can't believe I screwed up that [exam, case recitation, brief, oral argument, and so on] so horribly. Now the [judge, professor, my classmates, again, just fill in the blank] must think I'm a total idiot because I am. I should have done [fill in the blank]. I shouldn't have done [you name it.]"* Right then, **STOP SHOULD-ING ON YOURSELF!** Interrupt the hyper-dramatic parade of horribles that your ego in concert with your emotions cooked up. Again, subject what you are thinking to logic-based scrutiny. The person or persons you presume judged you so harshly have already forgotten about it and moved on. Now it is your turn to do the same.

You are your own worst critic. We all are. Your perception of how something went is apt to be distorted by the lens of your self-directed strict and harsh scrutiny. If you knew it all you would not be in school and you would likely be very, very old and living on a mountaintop somewhere in a remote region of the Himalayas. Give yourself a break and congratulate yourself for getting in the game. Know that even if you get knocked down, what matters is that you get back up. You are learning and getting better every day.

Most fear-based thinking is the product either of exhaustion or isolation.

Worry is a fear-based emotion. Most of our fears are born of exhaustion or isolation. If you are really tired, take a nap and then return to the task at hand. If you feel isolated, reach out to a family member or friend. Keep nurturing books close at hand, and turn to their chapters for a quick boost. Watch a few minutes of an inspiring speech or movie excerpt. Remember that although it will sometimes feel that way, you are never alone. There is a star that you are under, and life is rooting for you.

CHAPTER 51

How to Be When You Get Stuck in Negative Thoughts

Switch the thought.

When thoughts of gloom begin to set in, notice them and then **CHOOSE ANOTHER THOUGHT**. Keep in the forefront of your mind one particular experience from the past that made you happy. Conjure up its details. Feel it. When a self-defeating thought comes to mind replace it with that happy memory. Habituate the expression *"switch"* as your cue to switch up the thought.

Athletes employ sports psychologists who teach this "switch the thought" technique. A pitcher who needs to get his head back in the game or breakaway from fear will use a buzzword or phrase (*"switch"* or *"release the mechanism"*) to re-establish his positive focus. You do the same. You are in charge of your thoughts. Your thoughts are not in charge of you.

When you are feeling deflated, it is probably because you are holding yourself to an unrealistic standard.

When it all seems like too much, realize that you are most likely holding yourself to an unrealistic standard of perfection. Abandon the quest for some brand of nuanced excellence that you have conjured up and instead simply commit to *"good enough."* As long as your performance on the exam, the moot court exercise or the legal writing assignment is good enough, you will be fine.

To finish the race is to win the race. You do not have to come in first, second or even in the top 99%. The last one to cross the finish line still crosses the finish line. At your first trial, no judge will ask how you did in moot court. At your first closing, no client will pause to ask your Property grade. Every finish brings you closer to the dream. Take your time and cross the line.

When you feel stuck in a funk, simulate the body language of a really happy person.

Change your posture. Stand taller, shoulders back and chin literally up. Start smiling and laughing. I mean it. Start laughing really, really hard. It will seem nutty, but it works. Your brain's neurotransmitters will understand your smile and laughter to mean that you are really happy and in response release endorphins that will actually let how you feel match up with how you are acting.

I have a friend who teaches Laughing Yoga, a class where the members hold a posture and then laugh hysterically. I thought she (and they) were nuts, until she simulated a few minutes of the practice in our home. We all followed her instructions, stood in Warrior Two and then were led on a five-minute laughter explosion. The results were dramatic. Everyone's mood lifted and the various to-do lists seemed so much more achievable. By laughing at nothing, we learned to lighten up about everything. All the stuff that we get caught up in is not as important as we like to think.

CHAPTER 52

What to Do Before the Semester Ends

Read through your class notes to be sure that they are complete and clear.

Before the semester ends, run through your notes for each class. Jot down any questions or sources of confusion. Clear those up before the reading period, so that when you actually get down to the business of studying you won't be in the burdensome position of having to learn material from scratch. The study period should be spent reviewing, reducing the subject matter to an accessible format, and doing practice questions.

Think offensively about what is likely to be asked.

For each subject, think offensively about what is likely to be asked. By paying attention in class, you should get a good idea as to which topics have been stressed and which matters seem of particular interest to your professor. The student-teacher exchange should provide clues as to which sorts of answers the professor values. Ask each of your professors if he or she has any advice on exam-preparation and exam-taking. Listen carefully to the response.

If available, get copies of the professor's past exams.

Many schools make copies of past exams available on-line or at the reserve desk in the library. Take a look at those exams to begin to gauge the professor's likely expectations. After you have reviewed a given unit, find a former exam question that addresses that unit. Try to simulate exam conditions and do that question. Repeat that exercise as often as time permits. Ask your respective professors to comment on or critique your efforts. If the professor is unavailable, seek out the input of a legal writing specialist or tutor.

Make a study timetable.

Carefully review the exam schedule and set up a master study timetable for yourself. Budget and regiment your time. Build study breaks into the schedule. Build into the schedule things to look forward to. Keep the schedule handy and consult it often. It represents an important way for you to take control of the exam period and direct your energies.

CHAPTER 53

Getting Down to the Nuts and Bolts

Take the offensive.

To maintain a healthy, positive state of mind during exam time, take the offensive. So much of the anxiety that accompanies law school exam-taking resides in the sense that you are no longer in control, with forces beyond you now calling the shots. Accept your power and take back control. You can take matters into your own hands by understanding more about the skills that are tested on law school exams.

Be mindful of the skills that are tested on law school exams.

An objective exam (multiple choice, typically) is testing on your mastery of the subject matter as well as your powers of discernment. You want to be able to know which answer choices to eliminate and when to select *"all of the above"* or *"none of the above."* The best way to hone those aptitudes is by practicing the format in which the exam questions will be asked. Check with your teacher to see if past exams are available on-line. See if a study aid or workbook that contains comparable practice questions is available.

Studying for an objective exam will require lots of memorization. Even if the exam is open-book, you are unlikely to have the luxury of time within which to peruse your books and notes to uncover the right answer. Have the answer in your mind's eye, and then, if the exam is open-book and time permits at the end, use the resources that you brought in to double-check your work.

Use mnemonics, acronyms, metaphors and imagery to help you to memorize the essentials. Use index cards to test your memorization of the material. Write out the key points in longhand, rather than using your keyboard. Studies show that the process of actually writing down the material helps to anchor it more effectively than typing it.

Law school essay exams ask that you use your writing and analytical abilities (skills that you already possess) to apply the law that you have learned to various fact patterns, called hypotheticals. You will be graded on your ability to spot the relevant issues, discard the irrelevant issues and articulate the points and counter-points raised by the given hypothetical that is presented. Essay exams require that you use your writing and analytical abilities to answer the questions presented. Again, study for an open book exam the same way that you would study for a closed book exam. Memorize relevant essentials and, in advance of the exam, think about how the various topics that were covered relate to each other. Ask if the professor has copies of past exams available for review.

Law school essay exams test on the student's ability to be issue-inclusive and comprehensive. For purposes of grading, your professor will have prepared a master list of all of the topics and issues that the given question was intended to raise. She will have assigned point values to each of those topics. Your exam will suffer point deductions for every issue that you neglect to mention. Thus, you want to be as issue-inclusive as possible without including extraneous or irrelevant material.

Prepare an outline for each of your courses.

The outline that you prepare for each of your classes will prepare you to spot the issues on your exam and give those issues their due. Do not fall prey to the illusion that an "outline" is some mysterious and elusive document. An outline is simply a summary of the course, organized by topic, to help you to anchor and memorize key information. Create an outline to help you to see the connections between and among the units that you covered in class.

To prepare your outline, have by your side your casebook, a full and complete set of class notes and a good study guide. It is helpful too to have a copy of an upper class student's outline for the course, to serve as an example but not as a substitute for your own work. Use as that model an outline from a student who did well in the course and who had the same professor that you now have.

Using your syllabus and your casebook's table of contents as your guide, begin building your outline. Organize it according to headings and subheadings. For example, in Property, your course might begin with the acquisition of property other than by voluntary transfer. Hence, your outline might look something like this:

Unit One: The Acquisition of Property Other Than By Voluntary Transfer

1. **The Rule of Capture.** Here, you would state the rule. *One acquires a right to a wild animal by so mortally wounding it or ensnaring it as to render its escape a virtual impossibility.*

   A. **Leading case:** *Pierson v. Post.* Include a thumbnail sketch, in two or three sentences, of the case. For example, Post was in hot pursuit of a fox when Pierson, an interloper, stepped in and fired the fatal shot and hauled the fox away. Relying on ancient sources, the court crafted the rule of capture and awarded the fox to Pierson. The dissent would have submitted the matter to a panel of sportsmen or experts to decide.

   B. **Policies served by the rule:** It tries to impose a bright line, thereby fostering predictability and helping future prospective litigants to predict outcomes while also encouraging the eradication of a menace (the pesky fox).

   C. **Problems with the rule:** Here, you would note the rule's fuzzy edges. For example, what does "virtual impossibility" mean? Further, the rule encourages bad sportsmanship by rewarding spoilers. Moreover, the rule has led to overexploitation of natural resources and wildlife, preoccupation with capture technology and ecological devastation in some regions.

   D. **Points emphasized in class:** Here, note the variations on the rule and observations about the rule that class discussion prompted. Perhaps your class discussed *ratione soli,* meaning that a different result would have been reached in *Pierson v. Post* if the parties had been trespassing on the land of another. *Ratione soli* means that in the absence of an agreement to the contrary, resources found or hunted on private land belong to the landowner. Maybe your professor emphasized how the rule of capture applies to the acquisition of fugitive resources like gas or water. In class, be an active listener and carefully jot down the emphasized dimensions of the topic.

Condense your outline into a mini-checklist.

Once your outline is complete, condense it into a five to ten page mini-checklist of bullet points, again organized according to topic. Memorize the mini-checklist. When an exam is closed-book, go through that checklist in your mind's eye to be sure that you are being sufficiently issue-inclusive. On an open-book exam, you can turn to it but do not fall into the trap of thinking that you will have lots of time to peruse it. Know it so well that you do not need to spend much time looking at it, even when that option is available.

Study for open-book and closed-book exams the same way.

Do not fall into the trap of thinking that on an open book exam you will have the luxury of combing through your outline and other allowed materials to find answers. Exams are time-pressured. Study for an open-book exam in the same way that you would study if you were allowed to take no materials into the exam room. Even in statutory courses like Tax or Commercial Transactions, know the code sections before going into the exam. Use your statutory text, if it is allowed into the exam, as a back-up to consult to double-check your answers.

CHAPTER 54

Exam Preparation's Seven Points of Light

1) Be true to the study techniques that have worked for you in the past.

You know what works for you. Play your game, not someone else's. While the law school exam is different in form, it requires that you apply the same skills that got you into law school in the first place—good writing, reasoning, and analytical abilities. Do not abandon your own tried and true techniques for studying.

2) Avoid comparisons to others.

If you keep looking over your shoulder, you will trip over what is in front of you. What others are doing or not doing is their business. Your business is to stick to your tried and true study methods and do what must be done.

3) Avoid overkill.

The temptation, especially first year, is to get your hands on every possible hornbook, study aid, and outline that you can find.

Resist that temptation. Simplify. All you need is your casebook, class notes, one good sample outline, copies of past exams, and, if helpful, one good commercial study aid or outline.

4) Abandon any perfectionistic tendencies that you may have.

Many lawyers and lawyers-to-be suffer from the perfectionist syndrome. Strive for excellence, not perfection. Even better, remind yourself that you only need to pass. In the semesters ahead there will be many opportunities apart from exams for you to distinguish yourself. You will take advantage of those, thereby diminishing the significance of grades.

5) Repetition is the key to mastery.

The more you go over the material and the more times you review past exams the more proficient you will become. That proficiency will conquer your anxiety and help you to relax.

6) Performance is enhanced by calm.

Cognitive learning specialists tell us that retention, understanding and performance are enhanced immeasurably by calm. There are many hours in a day, and you have the time that you need. Keep matters in perspective. When all is said and done, you will be a lawyer. Not an A or B or C lawyer, but a lawyer.

7) Regardless of the grade, the studying itself is important.

No matter the result, you are not studying simply to do well on the final. The studying itself is important because you are learning for the sake of your life's craft. To think that you are studying solely for the sake of an exam is akin to a medical student's thinking that she needs to learn anatomy only to get through the final. Just as the future doctor had better know a pancreas from a gallbladder, the future lawyer will need to know a covenant from an easement. Moreover, the studying itself matters because you are honing aptitudes and developing proficiencies with every task that you accomplish. You are building intellectual muscle, and you will use that muscle to be strong in the world.

CHAPTER 55

Exam-Taking: Writing a Good Essay

Budget your time.

Often, your professors will let you know the format of the exam in advance. When that is the case, know how you will budget your time before going into the test. Once there, adhere to that time budget no matter what. When it is time to move on to the next question, move on. Your job is to finish the exam. Your grade will suffer mightily if you cannot devote the allocated time to each section of the test.

If you have not been told of the exam format in advance, once the exam is distributed take a few minutes to read the instructions to determine how many questions are presented and how many points are allocated to each. Create a time budget and stick to it.

Read the fact pattern like a detective searching for clues.

You are being tested on your ability to apply the law to facts in a thorough, issue-inclusive way. You want to read the fact pattern that is presented as if you were on a scavenger hunt looking for treasure or as if you were a detective looking for clues. The more issues you spot the better. Usually, every fact in the given fact pattern is there for a reason. As you read the question the first time, make notes in the margins indicating which issues you have spotted. Read the question a second time, and begin to quickly outline your response. As you are writing your answer, refer back to the question often to be sure that your understanding of the facts is correct. As you do that, issues that you did not spot immediately will become apparent.

Do not restate the facts for their own sake.

As you write your answer, include the facts that are salient to your determination. Do not, however, waste time by including in your answer a "recap" of the entire fact pattern. Your professor knows the facts. He or she wants you to be able to pull out relevant facts and link those to the legal issues presented.

Know the call of the question.

Most law school exams will present you with several hypotheticals, or fact patterns, and ask that you do something with those fact patterns. What you are asked to do with the facts presented is called the call of the question. It comes at the end of the fact pattern, and is usually in bold. For example, you might be asked to assess a particular party's claims against another party, or prepare a memo to a senior partner in your law firm outlining the issues involved. It is important that you pay attention to the call of the question before you begin to organize your response. Otherwise, you could find yourself answering a question that was not asked, without sufficient time to get to the question actually presented.

When answering an essay question, be issue-inclusive but do not include extraneous material.

For each essay that you write, be as issue-inclusive as possible. For example, imagine that you have been given an abbreviated amount of time within which to fill your wagon at Target or Wal-Mart's. The store (a metaphor for the given course) is vast. You must fill your wagon (your exam) quickly with items from the shelves (the issues being tested). You must be efficient and sufficiently inclusive to be sure that your wagon is chock-full, but also discerning to be sure that you have not included unnecessary items such as pet food when you have been asked to shop for apparel.

For each issue that you raise, anticipate and state the likely defenses or rebuttal. To continue with the shopping metaphor, if you have been asked to shop for clothing, include athletic socks and then indicate why dress socks might be appropriate. Make value judgments as to the efficacy or worthiness of each claim and defense. For instance, given plaintiff's athletic proclivities and preferences, indicate that dress socks seem a less worthy clothing choice to pursue. Throughout, state which additional facts you would need to learn to round out your answer.

Address only the issues that the facts present. There will be plenty of those. Do not lose time by digressing, going off on tangents or inserting extraneous material for its own sake.

Use headings to add organization and cohesiveness to your responses.

Organize your answers according to headings (and even sub-headings) for each of the subject areas that the question touches on. For example, on a Property exam your headings might look like *The Law of Finders, Adverse Possession, Concurrent Estates* and so on. Within the heading *Concurrent Estates* you might have sub-headings, such as *The Form of Co-Ownership: The Joint Tenancy, Co-Tenants' Rights and Duties* and so on, depending on what the facts of the given question happen to be. Under the heading *Landlord-Tenant Issues* you might use sub-headings such as *The Term of Years, Implied Warranty of Habitability, Covenant of Quiet Enjoyment, Duties of Assignee* and so on.

Remember that your job in answering an essay question is to address only the issues that are raised by the fact pattern that is presented. Do not include extraneous information or recite a run-on narrative for its own sake. For example, on a Property question if you discern that the parties are joint tenants, state so under the *Concurrent Estates* heading. Do not, however, pause to add that there are two other forms of co-ownership, the tenancy in common and the tenancy by the entirety. That is extraneous, irrelevant and will cost you precious time. If in that same question the facts present the opportunity to discuss a co-tenant's duty to refrain from committing waste, state so, but do not recite the list of other rights and duties of co-ownership for their own sake if they are not raised by the fact pattern.

Put each heading in bold, to give your professor a helpful roadmap to your answer as well as lend an internal cohesiveness to your response. If you are running out of time, be sure to include, if only in bullet points, the additional issues that you spotted but won't be able to elaborate upon.

For each issue, use IRAC: Issue, Rule, Analysis and Conclusion.

Under each heading, state the issue that is presented. For example, under *Concurrent Estates* one such issue statement might sound like, *"The issue presented is whether Gladys, who owns the land as joint tenant with her brother Jack, is responsible for her fair share of the costs of necessary repairs."* After you have stated the issue, state the rule of law that applies. For example, *"One joint tenant must pay his or her fair share of the costs of necessary repairs, provided that she was notified in advance and as long as the repairs are reasonable."* After you have stated the rule of law, engage in a fact-specific analysis of its potential application. For example, *"Here, Jack did notify Gladys of the need for the repairs, and it seems that he completed them in a reasonable manner."* Then get to your conclusion. For example, *"Thus, Gladys is liable to Jack for her fair share of the repair costs."*

This approach is known as **IRAC**, an acronym for issue, rule, analysis and conclusion. Use **IRAC** for each issue that appears. State the issue, state the rule of law that applies to help to resolve that issue, analyze the rule by applying it to the specific facts that are presented and state your conclusion. Anticipate that the analysis section might be quite quick for some issues and quite extensive for others.

To be sure that you are linking the rule of law that you have stated to the given facts presented, liberally use words like *"here"* or *"in this case."*

In addition to testing your ability to be issue-inclusive, law school essay exams are testing on your capacity to apply the law to facts. After all, that is what lawyers are required to do all the time. To be sure that you are not only stating the relevant rules of law but also focusing on how they apply to the facts at hand, frequently use words like *"here"* or *"in this case."* Those are bridge words, building the connection between law and facts.

Throughout, think about and state which additional facts you would need to learn.

Most questions cannot contain every relevant fact. Further, there may be nuances that are worthy of consideration but still unknown. State which additional facts you would need to learn, or would like to learn, and why.

Make value judgments and use common sense.

Think about the policy considerations at stake. Ask whether the course of action that is available is the most prudent course. No matter that the client has the right to do it, is it the right thing to do? Is the litigious course advisable? Are there alternatives?

Do not be informal in tone and do not try to be humorous.

Humor is risky and likely to detract from the integrity of your response. Be formal in tone throughout. Avoid colloquialisms and be respectful in tone.

CHAPTER 56

Ten Quick Tips to Avoid Common Exam-Taking Pitfalls

Exam-taking is a skill that improves with time and practice. To enhance your performance, keep in mind the following tips, intended to help you to avoid common, easily-remedied mistakes.

1) Be sure to answer the call of the question.

The call of the question is what the exam is asking you to do with the given fact pattern. It typically appears at the bottom of the hypothetical, often in bold print. For example, you might be asked to *"Determine Jane's rights and remedies as against Jake."* Answer the question(s) asked. Do not answer questions that are not asked. Do not waste precious time on tangents. Often, a student will lose points simply because he or she overlooked part of the call of the question, and failed to respond to one or more of the points asked.

2) Be issue-inclusive.

Spot as many relevant issues as you can. For each issue presented, note the relevant facts as well as any countervailing or competing considerations. For example, on a Property exam, if you are analyzing a restriction on land as an easement, also consider whether that same restriction could or could not be construed as a real covenant, or perhaps an equitable servitude, or maybe a mere license.

3) Follow through and define relevant legal doctrine.

Be sure to articulate the elements of all relevant causes of action. Define pertinent doctrines or concepts. For example, if the exam presents a nuisance issue, in answering, first define the nuisance. There, you might begin by noting that *"Jane should proceed against Jake for nuisance. Private nuisance is the substantial and unreasonable interference with another's interest in land."* Proceed to apply the exam's facts to the legal standard. You are being tested in considerable measure on your ability to apply salient legal doctrine to facts. Be sure to link your statement of the law, then, to the relevant facts presented. A helpful way to remember to do this is by resorting frequently to the word *"here."* For example, *"The elements of adverse possession doctrine require that the possessor's use be continuous. **Here**, Jill's possession was interrupted for six months."*

4) Organize your response.

Take time to outline and organize your answer. The use of headings can be very effective. Ultimately, the substance of your answer is far more important than its form. But a cogent, orderly, and organized format is a great plus. For that matter, if you hand-write your exam be sure to write legibly. To enhance overall readability, skip lines and write on every other page.

5) Do not restate the fact pattern.

Do not recount or summarize the fact pattern for its own sake. Your professor knows the fact pattern. He or she wrote it. Instead, be sure to apply the law to the facts presented. Selectively incorporate the relevant facts, connecting them to the applicable rule of law, theory and doctrine.

6) Do not present vague, run-on kitchen sink narratives of the law.

Unlike many college exams, you are not being asked to provide a treatise-like recitation of a whole body of doctrine or theory. Avoid any generalized discussion. You are being tested on your ability to spot the relevant issues and apply the law to the pertinent facts in an organized and concise manner.

7) Be a good lawyer.

As you sit down to take the exam, declare to yourself, *"I am a good and wise lawyer."* A good lawyer must make value judgments, sift the relevant facts from the irrelevant, and respond ethically and professionally. Think about your most positive legal role model. It might be a particular judge or attorney whose work you admire. It could be a fictional character. Internalize that person or character's best attributes and reflect those on the exam.

8) Do not surrender your common sense.

Think about and note the practical implications of the result that you are exploring. Make value judgments, such as *"This is plaintiff's weakest argument," "This is the issue that most favors the defendant," "I would not advance that cause of action because it is almost sure to fail," "Initiating this claim is apt to burn bridges between the parties"* and so on.

9) Budget your time and do not exceed the recommended time limit for each question.

This is perhaps most important of all. Carefully establish a time budget for each exam and honor that budget. You will be penalized for failure to get to a question. Force yourself to move on once the allotted time for a given question has run out.

10) Once the exam is over, let it go and move on.

Do not get weighed down by second-guessing yourself or doing *post-mortems,* particularly when you have another exam to prepare for.

CHAPTER 57

When It All Seems Like Too Much to Do

It does not have to be perfect.

When it all seems like too much to do, realize that is probably because you are holding yourself to some unrealistic standard of perfection. Abandon the quest for some brand of nuanced excellence that you have conjured up and simply commit to *"good enough."* As long as your performance on the exam, the moot court exercise or the legal writing assignment is good enough, you will be fine.

To finish the race is to win the race.

You do not have to come in first, second or even in the top 99%. The last one to cross the finish line still crosses the finish line. Many factors beyond grades will assure your success. Your attitude, passion, drive and determination are the best predictors of your future.

Trust that it will all be worth it.

Even if it seems a leap of faith right know, believe that you will be a very happy lawyer and that you will enjoy the rewards of a life well lived. Believe it because it is the truth about you and your chosen profession. There is a force that meets good with good.

Be a counter of blessings rather than a collector of grievances.

Cultivate a persistent attitude of great gratitude. You have been given a chance that most people around the world would do anything to have. When thoughts of gloom begin to set in, notice them and then *switch the thought*.

When a self-defeating thought pops up, *choose another thought.*

Keep in the forefront of your mind one particular experience from the past that made you feel successful. Maybe it was a graduation day, an outstanding performance on your part or some context in which you felt confident and in control. Remember it with as much detail as you possibly can. When a self-defeating doomsday thought comes creeping in, replace it with that happy memory.

You are in charge of your thoughts. Your thoughts are not in charge of you.

When panic or dread comes up, notice the thought that immediately preceded it. Test the veracity of that thought. By critically examining the thought that lead you to feel overwhelmed, you are switching from emotion mind to rational mind. That is good. In your rational mind, ask whether that thought is true. For example, suppose that you realize that the thought that precipitated your feeling swamped and exhausted was, *"I'll never get all this done,"* or *"I'll never understand this."* Those absolute, blanket characterizations tell you that you are in emotion mind, and your emotion mind can be a liar.

Remember that feelings are not facts. They are often fear-based and irrational. Instead of indulging those internal terror mongers, think, *"Baby steps. I can move this mountain even one inch at a time. When I get to material that I don't understand, I will mark it and later call a classmate or, if time permits, ask the professor about it. My work doesn't have to be perfect. I just need to pass, and I can do that. I will stick with this for the next two hours, and then I am going to watch How I Met Your Mother reruns and eat peanut butter cup ice cream."* Your energy level will perk up after that pep talk. Do what you promised yourself you would do, and then take that break.

CHAPTER 58

Once the Exam Is Over, Let It Go and Move On

Let it be.

Most of us who are drawn to the law have temperaments that make it difficult for us to let things go. Our tenacity can be a blessing, but sometimes it does not serve us well. When it comes to exams, once the exam is over *let it go*. Do not engage in *post mortem* de-briefing with classmates. Most often, that will make you feel unsure of what you did or did not do. Do not waste time after an exam by going back to your books to double check your responses. Move on, particularly if you have another exam to prepare for.

When you start to get pangs of anxiety over what you think you did or did not do on the exam, switch the thought. Say to yourself, *"No, no, no, I like you too much to have you beat yourself up right now."* And then resume your focus on the task at hand.

The ring around the bathtub remains.

Think of exam preparation as filling a bathtub. The water represents all of the information and material that you need to get into your head to get through the exam. When the exam is over, unplug the drain and let the tub empty. What remains is the ring, or core essentials that will stay with you for years to come. You must empty the tub to be able to fill it for the next exam. Do not let the old water stagnate. Let it go.

CHAPTER 59

On Grades

You are not your grades.

No grade has the power to define you, chart your course or set your limits. Only you have that power. Decide that the world is yours, and it is.

Law school modes of evaluation leave much to be desired. In a context where there is so little feedback, how one happens to do on a particular day on a three or four hour test tends to take on an undeserved importance and magnitude. Some even construe their grades as the final word on their abilities and opportunities as a future lawyer. Nothing could be further from the truth.

Your grades, whatever they happen to be, are an indication of how well you fared for a few hours in applying your learning to a narrow, often peculiar format, as determined by an inevitably arbitrary and usually subjective judgment. In this imperfect system, injustices and unexpected outcomes are inevitable. People who hardly studied may excel. The course that you thought you aced could represent your worst grade. The exam that you thought you bombed could come back as your best grade. And so on.

Let your grades inform your life, not define, diminish or even exalt it.

You are not your grades. Do not, even for an instant, submit to the misperception that any grade defines who you are and what you are capable of. To see how crazy that would be, imagine that you are told that you will be tested and graded on the sweater that you choose to wear on a particular day. The instructions indicate that the sweater should be in a primary color. You come to the "test" wearing a bright blue sweater. You thought about that choice in advance, and it seemed appropriate. You are graded on that choice, and the grade comes back a B-. When you ask why, you are told that wearing red would have earned you more points, and that sweaters with buttons fared better on this test. That B- does not tell a "truth" about you, your ability to dress yourself or your capacity to follow instructions. It does not even reveal any "truth" about the "worthiness" of the sweater that you picked. It is a perfectly good sweater. At best, giving the testing process every benefit of the doubt, it tells something about the merits of your sweater choice on that particular day. More likely, it indicates that the grader in subjective judgment prefers red to blue in the palate of primary colors.

Do not give any grade a significance that it does not deserve. Think of each grade as someone's opinion about the choices you made on a particular day. There are few absolutes in this realm, few wrong choices and certainly many opportunities to be self-corrective. You will get better at exam-taking the more times that you have the opportunity to go into the metaphorical closet and select a sweater.

Repetition is the key to mastery.

Grades are simply a means of feedback, letting you know whether you have figured out how to play the exam-taking game. If your grades are not what they should be, take the offensive, seeking out people and resources to help you to improve your exam skills. Consult with each of your professors. Find a tutor. Speak with upper-class students who have done well in the given courses you are now preparing for.

A few weeks before the semester ends, begin taking practice exams. Most of your professors will have their past exams on file. Ask your teachers to critique your work on those practice tests. That process, albeit tedious, is immensely helpful first because it hones your "muscle memory," or your brain's capacity to store and then more readily access the skill set needed to perform well on the actual test. Second, by receiving your professor's comments, you get a better sense of what he or she values most and deems most essential.

Diversify your portfolio.

You have the power to dilute the significance of grades by demonstrating your excellence in other contexts. Write on to a journal. Participate in moot court competitions. Do a judicial internship. Become a research assistant to a member of the faculty. Participate in a clinic. Those are among the ways for you to create value, establish yourself as a capable prospective practitioner, and shine.

To finish the race is to win the race.

As you do everything you can to enhance your performance, try to keep matters in perspective. Remember that the race is long and more like a marathon than a sprint. Pace yourself, and know that time is on your side. Be appreciative and grateful for the strides that you are making. Know that every step, however small, puts you that much closer to realizing your goal.

I promise you that on the occasion of your first deposition no one around that conference room table will turn to you and ask, *"By the way, what did you get in Evidence?"* At your first oral argument on a products liability case, the judge won't interrupt to inquire, *"So, how did you do in Torts?"* When you negotiate a pre-nuptial agreement on behalf of your client, you will not be asked, *"By the way, what was your Family Law grade?"* As you work on a corporate closing for an upstart company, its directors won't ask, *"By the way, how did you do in Tax when you took it in law school?"*

Think about the range of skills that you will apply to successfully handle a deposition, oral argument, negotiating session or corporate drafting meeting. That range is vast and will call on your intellectual *and* emotional quotients. That array of diverse aptitudes is not likely to be tested and graded on a law school exam. Grades, by definition, are a very limited indication of your vast repertoire of talents. Do not give them a power that they do not deserve.

In life, what counts is *who* you are. The multitudes of aptitudes and attributes that you bring are uniquely yours and have an important place at the table.

Only you create the reality that your grades represent. No one else can do that. Throughout, keep your head high. Hold tight to your dignity, integrity, and belief in yourself. You are precisely where you should be. You have succeeded before. You will succeed now.

Your brand of excellence will be uncovered, recognized and valued. But first, *you* have to value it. Do not denigrate your brand. Cherish it. Believe in it. Be proud of it. With quiet confidence, rest assured that the world will follow your lead.

Think, act and react as a successful, prosperous, and intelligent person would. Remember that what you think about most charts your path. Success is more attitude than it is aptitude. With your thoughts and attitudes, you are shaping the quality of your life.

CHAPTER 60

The Bar Exam

This too shall pass, and so will you.

The experience of preparing for and sitting for the bar exam represents a rite of passage and a bleak chapter in every new lawyer's lifetime. Fortunately, the process is temporary. This too shall pass, and so will you. Thereafter, trust that the rewards will come.

Throughout the process of studying, remind yourself often of all that you have achieved to have earned the entitlement to sit for the bar. Be proud of your accomplishments. You are a lawyer. The hard work has been done. You have earned the Juris Doctor. Now, you are seeking admission to a particular jurisdiction's bar. That is a privilege and an opportunity that countless others are denied. You are blessed beyond measure. Cultivate the presence of mind and spirit to see that.

When you hear yourself complaining, recollect the words of George Bernard Shaw, who said it best: *"Forget about the likes and the dislikes and do what must be done. For now, this is not about happiness. This is about greatness."* Greatness will be yours.

When preparing for the bar, remember that it is a pass/fail exam.

As you study, keep in mind that you are not aiming for excellence, and certainly not for perfection. You do not even have to do well. All you need to do is *well enough* to pass. This is a pass/fail exam. Thus, whether your performance is the equivalent of an A, B, C or D does not matter. A grade of D is a passing grade, and you only need to pass. Let that be a relief and a way for you to keep matters in perspective.

Fear is an illusion. Hard work is real.

Keep the fear factor at bay. Do not give the bar exam a mystique or *in terrorem* effect that it does not deserve. You have taken tests harder than this one and you have done well. Use the study methods that have worked for you in the past, put in the time and effort and you will succeed.

The three ingredients of successful bar exam preparation: generalize, memorize and keep doing practice questions.

There are three essentials to effective bar exam preparation. First, throughout your review of the material, generalize. Given the volumes of material that you are responsible for, all that you can and will be tested on are broad generalizations of law. Hence, resist your carefully honed lawyerly sensibilities to want to overanalyze and decline the temptation to dissect each point and study nuance.

Second, memorize those generalizations. The bar exam comes down to a memory game. You are being tested on your capacity to commit to heart a vast array of generalizations about various subjects. To anchor the material, use mnemonics, acronyms, imagery, metaphor, songs and whatever else you know works for you. No matter how corny, if it works, use it.

Third, keep doing practice questions. Repetition is the parent of mastery. You want to develop a conversancy with the peculiar format in which the questions are asked, and you want to practice answering those questions in that format again and again. That continued exposure will demystify the process and it will allow you to get better and stronger with each practice run.

The best is yet to be.

There is light at the end of this tunnel. You will bask in the well-deserved glory of a life well-lived. In the days ahead, do not let anything (including this exam) or anyone ever, even for an instant, convince you otherwise.

PART 8

How to Persist in Your Capacity to Love the Law

CHAPTER 61

The Pony

When I was in the sixth grade I was selected to participate in a national science fair. My project was based on the hypothesis that antibiotics could be grown from soil. I had several petri dishes filled with dirt, and mold and spores were growing in those plates. To try to figure out how those might become the stuff of penicillin, I had volumes and volumes of information piled up on the dining room table. Sifting through that material was tedious and often overwhelming. One night, as I sat there scratching my head, my dad must have sensed my growing despair.

My dad told me a story that he had heard on television. It is the story of a parent who has two children. One of the children is an avowed optimist, happy no matter the circumstances. The other is deeply pessimistic and cynical most of the time. The parent, trying to bring both children back to center, fills the pessimist's room with all of the toys and games known to delight even the fussiest child. He fills the optimist's room with several pounds of horse manure, to help to teach the child that sometimes life just stinks.

269

The parent waits ten minutes or so, and then ventures into the pessimist's room. He finds the child standing in a corner, arms folded in front of him, scowling. The boy says to the parent, *"How dare you patronize me with these petty offerings?"* Saddened, the parent heads to the optimist's room. There he is astonished to find his child busily spraying air freshener while shoveling the horse manure into a neat pile. The parent asks, *"Child, in the midst of all this, how can you possibly maintain so hopeful and cheerful an outlook?"* The child replies with great sincerity and strength of purpose, *"Daddy, don't you get it? With all this horse manure, there must be a pony here!"*

Do you see the analogy to your present circumstance? Amidst the volumes that you must shovel and store and sanitize, there are ponies. I promise you that. There will be joys and privileges in your chosen life's work that will astound and delight you. You have an important contribution to make, and it is uniquely yours. In the days ahead, do not let anyone or anything convince you otherwise.

Remember that life will meet you at your level of expectation for it. So will people. Keep your hopes high and look for the best in everyone and everything. It is there. Ask for the wisdom to see it.

To find love in the work that you do, put love into the work that you do. Tackle even the most mundane of tasks with the precision and grace of the greatest maestro. Write the memo, motion or brief with the assiduousness of Clarence Darrow. Prepare the case with the passion of the most fervent artists.

Make your work your art. Let others watch you with amazement as they ask, *"But why are you so happy?"* Smile and tell them, *"There's a pony coming."*

In Summation: Quick Reminders to Stay on Point as a Law Student and Lawyer

Lighten up. When you feel burdened by the weight of the world, realize that you are probably taking yourself too seriously.

In school, at work and throughout your lifetime you will get weighed down if you spend too much time worrying about what the grade will be or what others will think of you. Those worries are your ego talking. As my dear friend and colleague Andrea Schwartz often says, *"Your ego is not your amigo."*

Stop buying into the group-think that tells you that your performance on exams or at any given task will somehow determine the rest of your life. Even as I type those words, they sound ridiculous. The totality of choices that you make over the course of time will determine the rest of your life, not an exam, not a set of grades and not the outcome of any given assignment.

Remember that wisdom and compassion are indivisible.

Excellence cannot persist in the absence of kindness. Be kind. Respect intelligence, but respect decency even more. Everyone deserves respect, everyone has a story, and everyone has something to teach you.

Success is not the key to happiness. Happiness is the key to success.

Gratitude is the way to joy. No matter the adversity and incivilities that your life will sometimes be subjected to, you remain in charge of your reactions. A grateful heart does not have the room or the capacity to respond to meanness in kind. Cruelty comes from fragility. Gentleness comes from power.

A spirit rich in appreciation for everything and everyone twinkles. It refuses to internalize the slings and arrows, because it knows that the boomerang effect must return those to their sender. *People get what they give.* Thus, give what you want to receive. Remember that a grateful person will always have more to be thankful about. A critic will always have lots to complain about.

Love the law, and treat it as if you love it.

So urged Justice Cardozo in his address to New York University Law School's first graduating class. Love our craft, your work and the people in your life. Persist in loving the law, your work and people, even during those times when it seems that they do not love you back.

In life, you are who and what you love, and not who or what loves you. Love is always a choice. Choose it, again and again. Remember that the love part, at least at first, is easy. It is your capacity to persist in loving against all odds that will be the mark of your greatness.

What you think about and talk about most will grow.

However you define the world and your place in it, it will be just like that. Take care to seek out the good and to speak out the good. Be passionate and persistent in your praise of others. Be guided by what you admire and not by what you detest.

Look for the high-minded, read about the heroic, and talk about the acts of courage, big and small, that you observe. Speak the truth directly and with compassionate honesty, not brutal honesty.

Let the words that you choose promote understanding. Do not participate in gossip, mean-spirited humor or name-calling. Avoid sarcasm, which is weakness in disguise.

Avoid labels.

The imposition of a label (as in, my "opponent," "adversary," "liberal," "conservative" and so on), shuts the door to the world of variations, possibilities and surprises that your reserving judgment lets in.

You are not what you are called. You are what you answer to.

Take the time to answer for yourself the question, "Who do you think you are?" Otherwise, the world will jump in to answer for you. You are not an automaton, technocrat or hired gun. You are a champion of the underdog, a voice for those who have yet to find their own, a guarantor of due process and a crusader for justice. Answer to that.

The time to be happy is right now.

We are accustomed to delayed gratification and self-sacrifice for a greater good. Yet, in actuality, happiness is not the end but *the means* to that greater good. Your joy serves the world, and gives others' permission to express theirs. Keep close the people, experiences and things that bring you gladness.

Your life will take you to great heights. But no matter the altitude, honor your roots and be true to your first principles.

Remember who you are and where you come from. Honor the legacy that brought you to this place and time. Embrace a vision that deems the world noble and honorable. Urge others to awaken from the slumber of complacency and do what needs to be done with the time that they have.

By your example, teach that gentleness comes from strength. Know that you come to every room to heal the room. In the face of need and despair, you heal with one generous impulse rendered one day at a time.

You heal when you choose to love, and persist in loving the promise of the law and the clients, constituencies and causes that you are lucky enough to serve. Most of all, you heal when you finally decide to love yourself so much that the spillover cannot help but bring joy to the world.

A Closing Wish

My wish is that you wield the instrument of the law to close the gap between what is and what ought to be. The time is now to remember who you are and what you stand for and to show up, really show up, as a force for the good. Use your hard-earned expertise to give people hope. Because when all is said and done, if you can do that, well, that is something to be really happy about.